THE NEW
Newlywed
COOKBOOK

THE NEW
Newlywed
COOKBOOK

100 Recipes
for Every Couple to
Cook Together

KENZIE SWANHART

JULIEN LEVESQUE

ROCKRIDGE
PRESS

For general information on our other products and services or to obtain technical support, please contact our Customer Care Department within the U.S. at (866) 744-2665, or outside the U.S. at (510) 253-0500.

Rockridge Press publishes its books in a variety of electronic and print formats. Some content that appears in print may not be available in electronic books, and vice versa.

Interior and Cover Designer: Julie Schrader
Art Producer: Sara Feinstein
Editor: Bridget Fitzgerald
Production Editor: Andrew Yackira
Photography © 2019 Evi Abeler, cover, p.ii, vi-vii, x, 1, 19, 23, 60, 99, 104, 117, 133, 140, 153, 159, 171; Kenzie Swanhart and Julien Levesque, p. 128, 157, 179. Food styling by Albane Sharrard. Prop styling by Sara Feinstein. Author photos courtesy of © Lex Nelson Photography; Lace and Luce Photography.

ISBN: Print 978-1-64152-444-5 | eBook 978-1-64152-445-2

To our family, for always filling the dinner table with love and good food.

Italian Cheese and
Charcuterie Board,
page 158

CONTENTS

INTRODUCTION

CHAPTER ONE
A Kitchen for Two   1

CHAPTER TWO
Recipes for Two: Let's Stay In   18

» Breakfast & Brunch 19

» Quick Bites 40

» Dinner Dates 67

» Desserts for Two 104

CHAPTER THREE
Recipes for More: Easy, Practical Parties   120

» No-Fuss Cocktail Party 121

» Birthday Brunch 134

» Weekend BBQ 145

» Doable Dinner Party 156

» Friendsgiving Feast 168

Sauces & Extras   182

Measurement Conversions   186

The Dirty Dozen & the Clean Fifteen™   187

Index   188

INTRODUCTION

FROM A TINY CLOSET-SIZE KITCHEN in our first apartment to sprawling counters with plenty of room for all our kitchen supplies, we've been cooking together for as long as we've known each other. Our kitchen has grown and we have upgraded our pots and pans, but we will always treasure the memories we have made in every kitchen we have cooked in. Even when we lived in an apartment without a working oven, we danced around each other in the little galley kitchen while chopping veggies and preparing dinner—because cooking is, and always will be, special to us.

Our shared love of food—and trying and cooking cuisines from around the world—has become an important part of our relationship. When we decided to get married, we knew we wanted to do something out of the box for our wedding. We decided to bring our family and friends on vacation with us to the home of some of our favorite foods: Tuscany!

Our wedding was held in a thirteenth-century villa in the mountains of Tuscany on an estate covered in olive trees. It came as no surprise to those who know us that food took center stage throughout our wedding weekend. We forewent a traditional rehearsal dinner for a night filled with wood-fired pizza and prosecco for all our guests. On the big day, our cocktail hour featured a giant prosciutto carving station—and, at dessert, a personalized gelato cart in place of a cake. The entire wedding was far from traditional, and we wouldn't have wanted it any other way.

Now that we have tied the knot and are home, we are back in the kitchen creating new memories together with friends and family.

We are so excited to share with you a fresh approach to cooking for two that can work for any modern couple. From cozy date nights in to a weekend brunch for two, and even doable dinner parties, the recipes filling these pages are meant to ensure you and your partner grow your relationship through quality time in the kitchen, eat well, and, most importantly, have fun! This is not your grandmother's newlywed cookbook, and we don't want it left on the bookshelf collecting dust. We hope the spine breaks and the pages get splattered as you cook your way through the recipes. We want you to find your go-to weeknight dinners, favorite snacks and sides, and the dinner party menu you break out when you have loved ones over and want to really impress.

Spending time in the kitchen together is time we treasure because we connect and communicate in a special way. That is why we have specifically written these recipes for two people to cook together. If you decide to surprise each other with a meal, you can cook these recipes alone as well.

Throughout this book you will find a number of recipes for two: From quick, easy salads and 30-minute meals to decadent desserts, there's something for every taste. But we also love sharing our passion in the kitchen with our friends and family. We want to inspire you to spread love through food with ideas for practical parties, like a birthday brunch or Thanksgiving with friends (see pages 134 and 168, respectively). We'll also give you tips and tricks on what you'll need to set up your kitchen for success.

Welcome to *The New Newlywed Cookbook*—a new take on cooking for two. We hope you enjoy cooking through the recipes in this book as much as we enjoyed writing them!

1

A Kitchen for Two

Whether you have shared the kitchen for years or are outfitting your first home together, there are a few basics we want to offer to help you get started. Throughout this chapter we share our recommendations for how to set up your kitchen for stress-free cooking, which kitchen supplies you will need—and which ones you should skip—and how to organize all those new kitchen tools generously selected from your wedding registry. We will dive into the magic of cooking for two and how to entertain with ease. Most importantly, we will show you how to get the most out of this book and the delicious recipes inside it.

Remix the Registry

We were together for about eight years before we got married, and lived together for about six of those years. When we moved into our first apartment after college, we were lucky enough to receive a number of hand-me-downs from our families to outfit the kitchen. Over the years, and as cooking became the focus of Kenzie's career, we made small investments in the kitchen. Some purchases have turned out to be staples we use all the time, while others were impulse buys we could easily have forgone. There were also a few things we decided to wait on and place on our registry.

Following, we outline our recommendations for what a kitchen for two really needs. We also talk about the strengths and weaknesses of the standard wedding registry, what to register for, and what you will actually get. Whether or not you choose to register, we hope this helps you decide where to invest and what to skip when it comes to outfitting your kitchen.

WHAT YOU NEED

There are a number of common items that appear on just about every wedding registry, and most are small kitchen appliances and cookware. Whether registering for gifts or investing in new tools yourself, remember that quality products last longer and save money in the end. It doesn't matter if you're a kitchen novice or a budding chef: Quality cookware makes cooking each meal a pleasure. But you don't need to have a kitchen full of fancy tools to be a good cook. Following are our suggestions for which kitchen tools to set your sights on and which you should just skip.

CAST-IRON SKILLET: A cast-iron skillet is a must-have in every kitchen. We recommend a 10- to 12-inch pan if you are only going to have one. A cast-iron skillet has a naturally nonstick surface, heats evenly, and can be transferred to the oven—making it perfect for everything from crispy fried chicken to perfectly seared steaks. Additionally, a cast-iron skillet will last forever if you care for it properly. If you already have one or if you receive one as a hand-me-down when combining kitchens, you can leave this off the registry list.

DUTCH OVEN: From soups and stews to casseroles, whole roasted chickens, and even one-pot meals, an enamel-coated cast-iron Dutch oven is a kitchen workhorse. Not only are these pots sturdy enough to go from stove to oven, they are also pretty enough to transition right to your table. Just pick a size (or two) that will work best for your family.

FOOD PROCESSOR: This is a bit of a toss-up. With a food processor, you can get prep work done in no time—from shredding cheese to mixing dough for piecrust. You can also slice, dice, and purée in it. If you like to host, this is a must-have for large prep tasks, but if you plan mainly to cook for two, we recommend skipping the full-size version and opting for a mini food processor or chopper.

HIGH-SPEED BLENDER: The power and versatility of a high-speed blender are often overlooked. A high-speed blender can do so much more than just blend your morning smoothie. From smooth sauces to puréed dips and frozen desserts, a professional blender can do it all. We love our high-speed blender, which can also mill flour and make creamy nut butters. It can also be used in place of a juicer. Unless you're a juicing fanatic, don't waste precious counter space or registry real estate on a one-trick pony. From our point of view, a juicer is right up there with an avocado slicer or deviled egg tray. Skip these single-use items and fill your kitchen with versatile kitchen tools you are sure to use every week.

KNIVES: No kitchen should be without a good set of knives. However, while a full knife block looks great, it's not always necessary. To get started, all you really need are a chef's knife, serrated knife, paring knife, kitchen shears, and a knife sharpener. When choosing your preferred brand, look for stainless steel blades that run the length of the handle.

MULTI-COOKER: Slow cookers used to own the wedding registry, because who could say no to dinner waiting for you at the end of the day? Well, along came the electric pressure cooker and air fryer, and now they own the countertop. Register for one of each, or look for a multi-cooker that does it all. It is no secret we love our Ninja Foodi, the pressure cooker that crisps—and for good reason. The Ninja Foodi sears, sautés, steams, braises, air fries, bakes, roasts, pressure cooks, and more. It even makes rice!

POTS AND PANS: A set of sturdy pots and pans is a token item on many registries, but do you really need that 10-piece collection? Probably not. Choose a starter set from a professional-grade line. Investing in a 10-inch skillet, 3-quart covered saucepan, and 3-quart covered sauté pan or skillet will ensure that you can make just about any delicious dinner your heart desires. Look for pans that conduct heat well, like stainless steel with copper or aluminum cores. And while we know your first instinct is to go for the nonstick, stainless steel will give your food a restaurant-quality, golden-brown sear (plus it can go in the dishwasher, if you're lucky enough to have one).

STAND MIXER: This kitchen staple may already be on your registry, but how badly do you really need it? We think it's a toss-up. If you love to bake it is a must, as it tackles everything from cookie dough to whipped egg whites with ease. However, if you are a kitchen novice or only bake around the holidays, skip the stand mixer in favor of a small handheld electric mixer and other kitchen tools you will use every week.

WHAT YOU WANT

Whether or not you have an official registry, there are a few items that people love to give to newlyweds. These items can help round out your kitchen arsenal, and if you do register, consider adding a few of these to the list.

BAKEWARE: Most of us don't need the deluxe bakeware set. Instead, we recommend a few baking sheets, muffin tins, and a loaf pan. Toss the bent, burned pans you've been moving from apartment to apartment, and start fresh.

BARWARE: Whether you opt for an engagement party, shower, or another celebration, your registry can be ideal for items that will not only step up your kitchen, but also raise your entertaining game, such as barware. Look for a stylish and functional wine decanter, cocktail shaker, ice bucket and tongs, a jigger, and a bottle opener.

DISHWARE: Instead of picking out a china pattern, as your grandma may be urging you to do, opt for an all-purpose white dishware set you can mix and match with other dishes, linens, or serving pieces.

FLATWARE: To complement your dishware, select a solid flatware set. Trends come and go, so feel free to choose fun accent pieces but remember that a set of stainless-steel silverware will never go out of style.

STAND MIXER ATTACHMENTS: If you choose to register for a stand mixer, add a few accessories to your registry to get the most out of your new toy! (We especially recommend a pasta maker attachment.)

WINE GLASSES: If you are anything like us, this may be the most-used glassware in the cabinet. If you have the storage space and entertain often, register for a set that includes glasses for both white and red wine. Four of each type can handle a small impromptu party, or choose one classic all-purpose shape and stock up with 8 to 12—they break!

THE ULTIMATE ESSENTIALS

If you ditch the traditional wedding registry in place of a honeymoon fund, or are just moving in to a new place where you don't need a kitchen full of fancy tools to cook for two, there are a few pieces of equipment we consider essential.

CAST-IRON SKILLET: Equally useful for sautéing veggies and searing meat, this tool is a must-have for every kitchen.

CHEF'S KNIFE: This is the most important knife in the set. The chef's knife can be used for almost every task in the kitchen—from chopping, slicing, and dicing vegetables to slicing, cutting, and cubing protein.

CUTTING BOARDS: A selection of plastic and wooden cutting boards, in a variety of sizes for a variety of purposes, is a staple for every kitchen. Trust us, we know from experience. You probably won't want to ask guests if anyone brought along a cutting board big enough to carve the turkey you just cooked for your first holiday dinner!

MIXING BOWLS: Mixing bowls are used in almost every recipe. Opt for functional and pretty—we have a set of classic white bowls in a variety of sizes that can double as serving pieces.

NONSTICK PAN: While we often prefer a cast-iron skillet to sear and build flavor in our dishes, every kitchen needs at least one good nonstick pan for cooking eggs and pancakes.

SHEET PAN: Sheet pans are not a new kitchen gadget, but they have easily become one of our favorites. They are perfect for holding a lot of food, whether that's cookies or an entire sheet pan meal.

STOCKPOT: This simple kitchen vessel is essential for making soups, stews, and, of course, stock. Your pot should be large enough to cover a whole chicken and veggies with liquid, with room to spare.

Set Up Your Kitchen Like a Pro

Whether you have been cooking together for years or are ready to make your first meal together, we have a few tips and tricks to make the most of your time spent in the kitchen. After all, cooking together should be fun and should not feel like a chore! Setting up your kitchen for success can mean the difference between a delicious home-cooked meal and settling for takeout that you'll later regret.

If you already live together, a few tweaks to your kitchen organization and the ingredients in your pantry will ensure that you are always ready to whip up a quick snack or a last-minute meal. Take it from Kenzie, who cleans out, rearranges, and organizes the kitchen every few months: You will enjoy being in the kitchen more if it works for you.

ORGANIZATION

You may not have ever thought about this, or, if you know the concept, you may not realize it actually has a name: "The kitchen triangle" (a.k.a. "the golden triangle" or "the working triangle"), a concept going back to the early twentieth century, suggests that a kitchen's three main work areas (sink, stove, refrigerator) should form—yep—a triangle. Unfortunately, most kitchens don't follow this principle. In fact, every home in which we have lived together has had no triangle to speak of! Straight lines and wacky jigsaw puzzles created by galley floor plans and impeding islands have dominated our kitchen space, but we always make it work.

In today's home, the responsibility of preparing meals no longer rests squarely with one individual, which makes the kitchen triangle a bit of an outdated concept. Instead of focusing on the perfect triangle, set up kitchen zones that give each person in the kitchen a task and space to complete it. For example, your prep zone should have all the tools you need to prep a meal, such as cutting boards, knives, peelers, a food processor, and access to the trash bin.

If you love to bake, your baking zone, ideally near your oven, should hold all the tools you could possibly need to bake: measuring cups and spoons, bowls, a mixer, baking sheets, etc.

Simple things like placing cooking oils and spices near the stove, or storing flour and sugar in large Mason jars on the counter, ensures that everything you need is within easy reach.

Not all zones in the kitchen need to be for cooking. We have a coffee corner where we keep the coffeemaker, filters, mugs, and ground coffee. However, our glassware is split between the kitchen and dining room because we like to have our fancy wine and cocktail glasses by the bar cart and wine cabinet.

At the end of the day, your kitchen doesn't have to make sense for anyone but you. Try things for a few weeks and then move them around until it feels right.

PANTRY BASICS

Organizing your pantry may seem like a pretty straightforward task: Place newer items in back so you use older items before they expire, and make sure you can see everything—so you don't end up with eight cans of diced tomatoes. But what are the most important ingredients to keep on hand? Following is a checklist of some basic kitchen staples we always have in the fridge and pantry.

ALL-PURPOSE FLOUR: We keep a variety of flours on hand, since we have sufficient cabinet space. If you only have room for one type, make it all-purpose flour. Used for everything from biscuits and cookies to thickening sauces, this pantry staple lasts up to a year when stored in an airtight container.

BREAD CRUMBS: Perfect for topping casseroles and breading chicken. You can either buy packaged or save some money and make your own from slightly stale bread.

BROTH/STOCK: Broths and stocks are an easy way to add extra flavor to any recipe.

BUTTER: While we always have a stick or two of butter in the fridge, I also keep a few spares in the freezer—just in case. It'll keep for up to four months when frozen before its use-by date.

CANNED TOMATOES: Whether whole, diced, or puréed, tomatoes add acidity, sweetness, and color to a vast array of dishes. Canned tomatoes provide consistent flavor when fresh tomatoes are out of season.

DRY PASTA: Whether you prefer penne, rigatoni, or cavatappi, keeping dry pasta on hand means you are always prepared for an impromptu meal.

EGGS: A dozen eggs can come in handy for many meals at any time of day.

EXTRA-VIRGIN OLIVE OIL (EVOO): Just like flour, we keep a variety of oils in the pantry, but EVOO is the hero of most meals. A good olive oil can be used for everything: sautéing, finishing dishes, and everything else in between.

GARLIC: There are three staples we use in almost every recipe throughout this book: olive oil, sea salt, and freshly ground black pepper. If we had to choose a fourth, it would be garlic.

LEMONS: There aren't many fresh foods on our list of pantry staples, but having lemons available for fresh juice when cooking is a must.

LENTILS AND BEANS: Relatively inexpensive and super easy to make, lentils and beans add extra protein, fiber, and a bit of bulk to any dish.

ONION: Almost every great meal begins with sautéing an onion. Don't worry about keeping all varieties on the counter—a few yellow onions are versatile enough for most recipes.

PARMESAN CHEESE: A small amount packs a lot of flavor. Don't waste your money on pre-grated cheese: Buy a wedge to grate yourself, and it will last a while in the fridge.

SPICES: We could write a whole section on how to stock your spice cabinet, but there are a few staples you should always have on hand: sea salt, black pepper, basil, garlic powder, ground cinnamon, ground cumin, onion powder, oregano, and paprika.

WHOLE GRAINS: Rice, oats, and quinoa make satisfying bases for any meal and work for breakfast, lunch, dinner, and dessert.

PROS & CONS: BUYING IN BULK

These days, it seems we are constantly being told that more is more. Between buy-one-get-one sales and better deals for bigger quantities, it is particularly challenging for smaller households to buy exactly what they need without overspending or overbuying.

When shopping, stick to your grocery list and buy only what you actually need. Don't feel pressured by sales and family-size packaging to buy more than you need, or you will just end up wasting money when the food goes bad before you can use it all. In the produce aisle, you can get specific about the amounts you need, from bananas and tomatoes to Brussels sprouts and more.

That said, we do recommend checking out the bulk foods section—just don't feel like you need to buy large quantities! The bulk food aisle allows you to purchase dry goods such as grains, beans, nuts, and spices in the exact amounts you need, big or small.

Feed Each Other

Over the years, we have learned a lot about cooking for two. As we mentioned earlier, our first apartment right out of school had a kitchen the size of a closet. The two of us cooking together meant one of us was at the stove in the kitchen while the other chopped veggies in the living room.

With each new apartment, we gained a small amount of kitchen space. Now, we have a spacious kitchen with more than enough room to cook a weeknight dinner for two, or host over the holidays. As our space has changed, one thing has remained constant: focusing on simple but delicious recipes we cook together.

WHY COOK FOR TWO?

While most recipes you find online and gracing the pages of your favorite cookbooks are built for a family of four to six, we find that cooking for two allows us to try new things, focus on quality ingredients, and control what and how much we are eating.

We love food, so when we are not cooking at home, we are trying a new restaurant downtown or visiting local hole-in-the-wall joints that focus on food over fanfare. Then we take those influences back to our kitchen to recreate our new favorite dishes.

We've come a long way in the kitchen from our very first Valentine's Day together, where crazy college schedules necessitated an easy taco night (which we have recreated every year for almost the past decade). Working in the kitchen together, we have taught each other countless hacks, and we learn together as we try new cuisines.

LEFTOVERS: THE GREAT DIVIDE

There are two camps: leftover lovers and leftover haters. We are split down the middle in our home. Kenzie loves the convenience that leftovers provide for a quick and easy lunch, but Julien hates eating the same thing for more than one meal in a row.

While not all leftovers are created equal, there are ways to elevate extra food the next day. Instead of a microwave, use your stove and oven to bring life and texture back to your food. You can also repurpose proteins in new ways, using them as toppings for salads or transforming them into stir-fries. Use leftover rice to create a quick fried rice, or bake it into mini rice croquettes.

Get creative, but be sure to enjoy your leftovers within a few days. No one wants to be eating food past its prime!

ONE DISH, TWO (OR THREE) DINNERS

If you are like Kenzie and enjoy taking leftovers for lunch or planning ahead for dinner throughout the week, you can easily double the recipes in chapter 1 to serve four instead of two. Another tip is to cook larger cuts of meat that can be used to make multiple meals. Instead of roasting a three-pound chicken, roast a seven-pound chicken so you have leftovers for a quick salad or chicken tacos as a handy lunch. If you are making grains to accompany your meal, double the batch and you can toss together a hearty grain bowl when your partner is working late.

Feed Everyone

While we spend most of our time in the kitchen cooking with and for each other, we also love to share our passion for food with friends and family. From easy dinner parties with another couple to birthday parties and holidays with family, there is nothing more rewarding than spending time with the ones you love gathered around the table.

Hosting shouldn't be scary or intimidating, so we want to arm you with everything you need to entertain with ease. In the final chapter of this book, we share menus and recipe inspirations for eight different events.

THE LOST ART OF THE COCKTAIL PARTY

If you are new to hosting, try kicking things off with a cocktail party. It is the perfect intro to entertaining, because it is a casual event that is sure to pay off in a big way. On page 121 we offer a handful of no-fuss, make-ahead recipes for little bites that are festive and fun. Round things out with a signature craft cocktail and a good bottle of wine.

We love hosting cocktail parties before another event because there is always a designated end time. Try hosting a mixer before a formal dinner, play, or concert! You can also wrap the party around another event, like a game night with friends. We love gathering the group for a quiet night in with a deck of cards or a board game. Prep a few appetizers and a batch cocktail, and you are good to go.

DINNER PARTIES MADE EASY

Dinner parties sound intimidating, but the truth is they are totally doable! We love hosting because we get to spend time together in the kitchen and then time with our friends enjoying the fruits of our labor.

Sometimes we go all out with a theme, a fun table setting, and a four-course meal. Most of the time, we keep things simple and just enjoy a good meal with good friends. Either way, the keys to planning a stress-free dinner party are to pick a few crowd-pleasing recipes (check out chapter 3), prep ahead, and have fun. A good cocktail doesn't hurt either.

Remember to lean on each other and work together as partners when planning and prepping. This year, we made a joint New Year's resolution to host one dinner party a month. While we have missed one month and doubled up during others, we have really enjoyed spending time together planning the menu, trying new recipes, and eating good food with the ones we love.

Our biggest tip for keeping your cool while cooking for a crowd? Plan ahead and pick a recipe you know how to make. If you want to wow your guests with something new, take it for a test drive the week before. Nothing is worse than a recipe not going the way you want or forgetting an ingredient—believe us! We have made many last-minute runs to the grocery store for the special spice we forgot to buy or a backup pie when the soufflés fall.

HOW-TO: PARTY PREP

After you have picked the theme and decided on the perfect recipes for the party, it is important to scale your recipes so you have enough to feed everyone without having leftovers for a week (flashback to Friendsgiving 2015 when we had five pounds of leftover mashed potatoes!).

We can't decide which would be worse: running out of dinner or running out of drinks. Follow these simple rules to take the stress out of planning, whether you are hosting five or 50:

APPETIZERS: On average, each guest will have about six servings of appetizers, although this number may double if it's a cocktail party. Pro tip: Stock up on bulk items such as nuts, pretzels, and olives that guests can munch on when they arrive!

ENTRÉES: Plan for each guest to enjoy about six ounces of protein or four ounces of pasta.

SIDES: Depending on the type of side dish, guests usually consume two to four ounces, or less for salad. If you are serving buns or rolls, plan on one or two pieces per person.

DESSERT: No matter how filling dinner was, there's always room for dessert. Plan on one slice or serving per person.

DRINKS: When it comes to alcohol, one bottle of wine for every two adult guests or two beers per guest per hour is a good rule of thumb. If you are serving cocktails, plan for three drinks per person. Don't forget to account for nonalcoholic drinks—one drink per person if alcohol is provided, three per person if alcohol isn't.

When in doubt, or if you're coming up short, make a giant salad to accompany your meal, and pull out the extra bottles of wine you stashed in the closet.

About the Recipes

Before we dive into the actual recipes, we are going to outline how we structured the book and how we recommend you should approach the recipes throughout.

Whether you are planning something special or looking for a quick and easy 30-minute meal to solve the age-old weeknight question, "What's for dinner?," you will find the perfect recipe for every occasion.

Above all else, remember to have fun and grab your plus-one, because it's time to cook—together!

FOR TWO & FOR MORE

The following chapters are filled with simple, flavorful recipes specifically designed to be cooked by two people. You will find recipes for breakfast, snacks, and appetizers, as well as a variety of entrées and desserts—all for two. You will also find our favorite recipes to feed a crowd for those special dinner parties and holidays.

As you begin, remember to read each recipe completely and gather all the ingredients you need in advance. As with everything else, a little prep work before you begin to cook will save you time in the long run. We also suggest you follow each recipe exactly as written when first trying it. Then, as you become more comfortable, you can switch things up and try swapping ingredients.

We recommend starting with a recipe like our Prosciutto-Wrapped Chicken (page 68) or Classic Beef Stew (page 78); when you're ready for a challenge, try our Cacio e Pepe (page 91) or Mussels in White Wine & Garlic with Crusty Bread (page 96). And if you're reading this book a week before your housewarming party, flip directly to our No-Fuss Cocktail Party menu (page 121).

FOR THE SOUS CHEF

After years of cooking together, we have developed a shorthand in the kitchen to help us work in unison, dividing tasks so we complement each other rather than step on each other's toes—literally. But this only came after years of duplicating work and having ingredients ready at the wrong time. To help you ease into the idea of cooking together, we have included notes throughout the recipes on how you can incorporate a sous chef into the mix.

Pick a lead chef and a sous chef one night, and then switch the next so you both expand your skills in the kitchen. Eventually, you'll each discover your favorite recipes (or tasks). Luckily, Julien loves to do the dishes, so he keeps the kitchen clean as we move from one task to the next, while Kenzie loves to set the table and plate the food. The prep and cooking is split down the middle.

Remember, you can also prepare these meals as a solo cook. Surprise your significant other with breakfast in bed or take on dinner when they have had a particularly hard day.

LABELS

We have included a variety of labels to guide you through the recipes. You will find dietary labels (i.e., **DAIRY FREE, GLUTEN FREE, NUT FREE**) so you know which recipes fit with your lifestyle and which you can modify slightly to make work for you. You will also note the following labels to help you find the perfect recipe for every meal:

COZY COMFORTS: traditional, classic comfort food

DATE NIGHT: recipes that are a little more ambitious and romantic

MEATLESS MONDAY: perfect for Monday, or any night when you want something a bit lighter or prefer a vegetarian meal

ONE POT: requires just one pot to assemble and cook

WEEKNIGHT: main dishes that require under 30 minutes—start to finish

TIPS

Throughout the recipes, we have provided our most helpful tips and tricks so you can cook with ease and even elevate your dishes in a snap.

FOR TWO/FOR A CROWD: Easy ways to increase (in chapter 2) or decrease (in chapter 3) the recipe yields so you can share your favorite weeknight meals for two with friends and family, or vice versa.

INGREDIENT TIP: Here we share our depth of knowledge on specific ingredients, including details on selecting and buying ingredients, working with them, and storing them.

KITCHEN HACK: We've shared our best kitchen organization ideas, cooking shortcuts, and alternative tools to help prep the recipes.

MIX IT UP: This is where we help you customize the recipes to add a personal touch!

PREP TIP: All our time-saving tips to make prep work easier and cleanup quicker.

SWAP IT OUT: Making recipes your own is easy when you follow our recommendations for swapping ingredients in and out. These are our best ideas for changing up the flavor profile or subbing ingredients for allergy reasons.

2

Recipes for Two: Let's Stay In

Cooking together most nights of the week, we have definitely fallen into a few recipe ruts, making the same meals over and over. When this happens, we draw inspiration from a large number of sources, like local restaurants, family recipes, and online cooking videos. Between freestyling in the kitchen and adding creative twists to classic dishes, we have created quite the repertoire of recipes for two. We picked our favorites for this book (no easy task!), dusted off a few classics, and did the delicious work of testing and choosing the best of the best.

All the recipes in this chapter are special to us. Kenzie developed the recipe for Chicken & Chickpea Tikka Masala (page 70) specifically for Julien, letting him taste test every version. We cooked the Cacio e Pepe (page 91) on our anniversary. Julien always makes the Easy Chicken & Shiitake Ramen (page 69) for Kenzie when she is sick. We make the Homemade Crispy Waffles (page 33) almost every weekend. And Julien is known to pile leftovers of the Carnitas Tacos with Pickled Red Onion & Slaw (page 76) on salads, rice bowls, and more! We can't wait for you to begin cooking through these, and start new traditions together!

Breakfast & Brunch

HOMEMADE GRANOLA & YOGURT PARFAIT   **20**

EGGS BENEDICT FLORENTINE   **21**

TOMATO, SPINACH & GOAT CHEESE OMELETS   **24**

EGGS & BACON FRIED RICE   **26**

BREAKFAST SANDWICHES ON TOASTED BRIOCHE   **28**

CHOCOLATE HAZELNUT CREPES WITH FRESH STRAWBERRIES   **30**

MIXED BERRY DUTCH BABY   **32**

HOMEMADE CRISPY WAFFLES   **33**

FRENCH TOAST WITH PEACHES & HONEY   **35**

GIANT CINNAMON ROLLS   **37**

HOMEMADE GRANOLA & YOGURT PARFAIT

SERVES 2 | PREP TIME: 5 MINUTES | COOK TIME: 20 MINUTES, PLUS 45 MINUTES
COOLING TIME

Meatless Monday

Whether we are grabbing a bite to go or enjoying brunch at a trendy café, one of Julien's go-to breakfasts year-round is granola and yogurt. There are so many granola varieties you can pick up at the store—but you'll never want to buy them again after you see how easy it is to make at home!

1 CUP OLD-FASHIONED ROLLED OATS

¼ CUP PECANS

¼ CUP ALMONDS

⅛ TEASPOON SALT

⅛ TEASPOON GROUND CINNAMON

2 TABLESPOONS OLIVE OIL

2 TABLESPOONS MAPLE SYRUP

¼ TEASPOON VANILLA EXTRACT

1 CUP PLAIN GREEK YOGURT

¼ CUP FRESH BLUEBERRIES

¼ CUP FRESH RASPBERRIES

¼ CUP HALVED FRESH STRAWBERRIES

1. Preheat the oven to 350°F. Line a large baking sheet with parchment paper and set aside.

2. In a large bowl, stir together the oats, pecans, almonds, salt, and cinnamon.

3. Add the olive oil, maple syrup, and vanilla. Mix until all the dry ingredients are evenly coated. Pour the granola onto the prepared baking sheet, using a spatula to create an even layer.

4. Bake the granola for 20 minutes, stirring halfway through the baking time. Remove from the oven and let cool for at least 45 minutes.

5. Use your hands to break the granola into pieces. Divide it into two equal portions, storing half in an airtight container.

6. Divide the yogurt into two bowls. Add half of the blueberries, raspberries, and strawberries to each. Top each bowl with half of the remaining granola.

For the Sous Chef

Preheat the oven and measure the dry ingredients. Once the granola is in the oven, wash the berries before halving the strawberries.

EGGS BENEDICT FLORENTINE

SERVES 2 | PREP TIME: 5 MINUTES | COOK TIME: 10 MINUTES

Cozy Comforts, Dairy Free, Nut Free

After our wedding, we were fortunate enough to continue celebrating our honeymoon in Italy. The hotel we stayed in offered an incredible breakfast spread—including perfectly poached eggs served with spinach and miniature crispy toasts. Our honeymoon-inspired take on eggs Benedict is a lighter version of this breakfast classic that you can whip up much more quickly than you might think!

1 TEASPOON EXTRA-VIRGIN OLIVE OIL

6 OUNCES FRESH SPINACH

SEA SALT

FRESHLY GROUND BLACK PEPPER

2 ENGLISH MUFFINS, SPLIT AND TOASTED

1 TEASPOON WHITE VINEGAR

5 EGGS, DIVIDED

3 TABLESPOONS MAYONNAISE

1 TABLESPOON FRESHLY SQUEEZED LEMON JUICE

2 TEASPOONS WATER

1. In a large skillet over medium heat, heat the olive oil.

2. Add the spinach and sauté for 3 to 4 minutes, until wilted. Season with salt and pepper.

3. Place both halves of a toasted English muffin on each of two plates. Top the muffin halves evenly with the cooked spinach.

4. In a deep skillet or large saucepan, bring 3 inches of water to a boil over high heat. Adjust the heat to keep the water gently simmering; add the vinegar.

5. Break one egg into a ramekin or small bowl. Gently slide the egg into the simmering water. Repeat with three more eggs—you will have one left.

6. Poach the eggs for 3 to 4 minutes, until the egg whites are firm. Using a slotted spoon, remove the eggs, placing one on each of the spinach-topped English muffin halves.

(Continued)

7. In a blender, combine the yolk from the remaining egg with the mayonnaise, lemon juice, and water; blend until smooth.

8. Gently spoon or spread the sauce on top of the eggs.

For the Sous Chef

While your chef is getting the spinach started, you can complete steps 3 and 4. Once the eggs are poaching, make the hollandaise sauce in step 7.

TOMATO, SPINACH & GOAT CHEESE OMELETS

SERVES 2 | PREP TIME: 5 MINUTES | COOK TIME: 10 MINUTES

Gluten Free, Meatless Monday, Nut Free

One of the many apartments we've lived in together was a half block away from an amazing diner in Boston called Mike's. There's always a line to sit on the weekends, but you're guaranteed to leave happy and full. Now that we don't live as close, we love bringing the taste of a weekend diner trip right into our kitchen with omelets like this one. With bright colors and flavors and a variety of textures, this omelet will become your new go-to for a quick and healthy breakfast.

5 EGGS

SEA SALT

FRESHLY GROUND BLACK PEPPER

1 TABLESPOON UNSALTED BUTTER, DIVIDED

3 TABLESPOONS SEMI-SOFT GOAT CHEESE, DIVIDED

1 CUP FRESH BABY SPINACH LEAVES, DIVIDED

1 MEDIUM TOMATO, DICED, DIVIDED

1. Heat a nonstick pan over medium heat.

2. In small bowl, combine the eggs, salt, and pepper. Using a fork, beat the eggs for about 1 minute or until the mixture is a consistent yellow color throughout.

3. Melt 1½ teaspoons of butter in the hot pan until it is foaming. Pour in half the egg mixture. Cook for about 1 minute, tilting the pan to allow the uncooked egg to shift and cook evenly.

4. Once the egg is mostly set with a slightly runny top, sprinkle one side of the eggs with 1½ tablespoons of goat cheese, ½ cup of spinach, and half the tomato.

5. Remove the pan from the heat and cover with a lid for 1 minute to cook the omelet and vegetables evenly. Once the eggs are fully set and the spinach is slightly wilted, fold the empty half over the cheese and veggies to complete the omelet.

6. Transfer the omelet to a plate, then repeat with the remaining ingredients for the second omelet.

KITCHEN HACK: For a perfectly plated omelet, ditch the spatula! Place your plate on top of the pan and carefully flip it to drop the omelet right onto the plate.

For the Sous Chef

While the chef is whisking the eggs in step 2, dice and divide the tomato, and divide the spinach leaves and goat cheese. If you have two nonstick pans, you could also begin the second omelet while the first one is still cooking.

EGGS & BACON FRIED RICE

SERVES 2 | PREP TIME: 10 MINUTES | COOK TIME: 30 MINUTES

Cozy Comforts, Dairy Free, Nut Free

One of Kenzie's favorite takeout guilty pleasures, when we've had a long day and want to indulge, is fried rice from a Thai restaurant in our neighborhood. And much to Julien's dismay, she also loves having breakfast for dinner! This recipe tackles both of those wants—and even Julien can't say no to this joining together of meals.

2 CUPS WATER

1 CUP UNCOOKED WHITE RICE

3 BACON SLICES

2 EGGS

SEA SALT

FRESHLY GROUND
BLACK PEPPER

½ YELLOW ONION, CHOPPED

½ CUP FROZEN PEAS

2 TEASPOONS SOY
SAUCE, DIVIDED

1. In a large saucepan over high heat, combine the water and rice and bring to a boil. Reduce the heat to medium-low, cover the pan, and cook for about 25 minutes, until the liquid is fully absorbed.

2. While the rice cooks, in a large skillet over medium-high heat, cook the bacon, turning every 2 to 3 minutes, until fully cooked, about 10 minutes total. Carefully transfer the bacon to a paper towel–lined plate to drain. Reserve the bacon fat in the pan. Once the bacon has cooled, crumble it into small pieces and set aside.

3. In a small bowl, combine the eggs, salt, and pepper. Using a fork, beat the eggs for about 1 minute or until the egg mixture is a consistent yellow color throughout.

4. Heat the skillet with the reserved bacon fat over medium heat. Pour in the eggs and cook, stirring, until they begin to set, about 2 minutes.

5. Stir in the onion, peas, and 1 teaspoon of the soy sauce. Continue to cook, stirring until the onion is translucent, about 5 minutes more.

6. Reduce the heat to low. Add the rice, crumbled bacon, and remaining 1 teaspoon of soy sauce, stirring until well combined.

> **INGREDIENT TIP:** To make this recipe gluten free, swap in gluten-free soy sauce or tamari.

For the Sous Chef

While your chef is finishing step 2, get a head start on step 3.

BREAKFAST SANDWICHES ON TOASTED BRIOCHE

SERVES 2 | PREP TIME: 5 MINUTES | COOK TIME: 15 MINUTES

Cozy Comforts, Nut Free, One Pot

Brioche may not be the first bread you think of grabbing if you want to make a breakfast sandwich, but this buttery French bread is the perfect vehicle for holding the eggs, cheese, bacon, and tomato in this recipe. The best part about these sandwiches? You can complete every step using the same pan for a quick and easy cleanup.

1 TABLESPOON UNSALTED BUTTER

4 THICK SLICES BRIOCHE BREAD

3 BACON SLICES

1 SMALL TOMATO, CUT INTO ¼-INCH-THICK SLICES

SEA SALT

FRESHLY GROUND BLACK PEPPER

2 EGGS

4 THIN SLICES SHARP CHEDDAR CHEESE

1. Heat a large cast-iron skillet over medium heat. Add the butter and let it fully melt.

2. Place the brioche slices in the pan and cook for 15 to 20 seconds, until they start to turn brown. Flip the slices and toast for another 15 to 20 seconds, then remove them from the skillet and place two of the pieces on individual plates.

3. Return the skillet to the stove over medium-high heat and place the bacon slices in it. Cook, turning every 2 to 3 minutes, until the bacon is fully crisp, about 10 minutes total. Carefully transfer the bacon to a paper towel–lined plate to drain. Reserve the bacon fat in the pan.

4. Place 2 to 3 tomato slices on each of two brioche slices and season with salt and pepper. Break the cooked bacon pieces in half and place three pieces parallel to each other on top of the tomato.

5. Return the pan to the heat. Carefully crack the eggs directly into the pan, allowing them to slip in so the yolks don't break.

6. Turn the heat to low and cook the eggs until the whites are completely set, about 1 minute. Gently flip the eggs and cook for 30 seconds more. Place one cooked egg on each bacon and tomato-topped brioche slice.

7. Top each with two slices of cheddar cheese and the remaining pieces of brioche to complete your sandwich.

SWAP IT OUT: If you'd like to make this recipe vegetarian, skip the bacon and use one additional tablespoon of butter to fry your eggs—and try adding some sliced avocado to your sandwiches!

For the Sous Chef:

Start by slicing the brioche and the tomato while your chef gets started on step 1. Then, tackle step 4 by starting to assemble the sandwiches so your chef can begin cooking the eggs in step 5.

CHOCOLATE HAZELNUT CREPES WITH FRESH STRAWBERRIES

SERVES 2 | PREP TIME: 5 MINUTES | COOK TIME: 10 MINUTES

Cozy Comforts

There's a tiny restaurant a few blocks from our home that specializes in crepes. They constantly have a crowd, and they have no fewer than 30 savory and sweet crepes on the menu! Our version keeps it simple with decadent chocolate-hazelnut spread and bright, juicy strawberries to satisfy your craving for a sweet breakfast choice.

2 EGGS

½ CUP MILK

½ CUP WATER

1 CUP ALL-PURPOSE FLOUR

¼ TEASPOON SALT

2 TABLESPOONS UNSALTED BUTTER, MELTED, PLUS 1 TABLESPOON

¼ CUP CHOCOLATE-HAZELNUT SPREAD (PAGE 183)

16 FRESH STRAWBERRIES, HALVED

1. In a large bowl, whisk the eggs and milk.

2. Gradually add the water and flour, whisking to combine. Add the salt and 2 tablespoons of melted butter and whisk until smooth.

3. In a large skillet over medium-high heat, melt the remaining 1 tablespoon of butter.

4. Measure ¼ cup of the crepe batter and pour it into the hot pan. Tilt the pan in a circular motion to ensure that the batter evenly spreads and coats the pan.

5. Cook for 2 minutes or until the bottom of the crepe is light brown. Using a large, flat, rounded-edge spatula, carefully loosen and flip the crepe. Cook the other side for 30 to 45 seconds, until fully cooked; transfer it to a plate.

6. Using a smaller spatula, spread 1 tablespoon of the chocolate-hazelnut spread onto one side of the crepe. Add 8 strawberry halves. Fold the crepe in half, then in half again, and serve.

7. Repeat until all the crepe batter is used.

> **MIX IT UP:** This batter is the perfect base for any kind of crepe. Try swapping the strawberries for bananas if you have a sweet tooth, or keep it simple by topping with some freshly squeezed lemon juice and sugar.

For the Sous Chef

Preheat the skillet and prep the ingredients by melting 2 tablespoons of butter and halving the strawberries. Complete step 6 while your chef is cooking and watching the crepes.

MIXED BERRY DUTCH BABY

SERVES 4 | PREP TIME: 10 MINUTES | COOK TIME: 20 MINUTES

Cozy Comforts, Meatless Monday, Nut Free

If you've never heard of a Dutch baby, imagine the outcome if a pancake, a crepe, and a popover had a (Dutch) baby! A little crispy on the edges, soft on the inside, and filled with beautiful berries, we promise you'll want to make this every weekend.

2 EGGS

¼ CUP SUGAR

¼ TEASPOON FINELY GRATED LEMON ZEST

⅛ TEASPOON SEA SALT

⅓ CUP ALL-PURPOSE FLOUR

⅓ CUP MILK

½ CUP FRESH RASPBERRIES, DIVIDED

½ CUP FRESH BLACKBERRIES, DIVIDED

½ CUP FRESH STRAWBERRIES, HULLED AND HALVED, DIVIDED

2 TABLESPOONS UNSALTED BUTTER

POWDERED SUGAR, FOR DUSTING

1. Preheat the oven to 425°F and heat a medium cast-iron skillet over medium heat.

2. In a medium bowl, whisk the eggs, sugar, lemon zest, and salt until fully combined. Add the flour and milk and whisk until smooth.

3. Add ¼ cup of raspberries, ¼ cup of blackberries, and ¼ cup of strawberries to the batter.

4. Melt the butter in the skillet and add the batter, ensuring the fruit is evenly spread throughout. Bake on the center rack for 20 minutes, until the edges are browned and risen and the center has begun to brown.

5. Remove the skillet from the oven and dust the Dutch baby with powdered sugar.

6. Serve with the remaining berries on top.

For the Sous Chef

Start by getting the oven and skillet ready in step 1. Then hull and halve the strawberries while your chef is making the batter in step 2.

HOMEMADE CRISPY WAFFLES

MAKES 5 OR 6 WAFFLES, SERVES 2 | PREP TIME: 15 MINUTES | COOK TIME: 15 TO 18 MINUTES

Cozy Comforts, Meatless Monday, Nut Free

Waffles are a favorite in our house, because you can completely change the flavors just by mixing up the toppings you use. While Kenzie is a "waffle traditionalist" with a preference for simple butter and syrup, Julien likes to get a little crazy with fruit and whipped cream. Whatever we're finishing off our waffles with, this recipe gives you a crispy outside with a fluffy inside—the best of both worlds!

1 CUP ALL-PURPOSE FLOUR

1 TEASPOON BAKING POWDER

½ TEASPOON BAKING SODA

¼ TEASPOON SALT

1 CUP MILK

4 TABLESPOONS UNSALTED BUTTER, MELTED

½ TEASPOON VANILLA EXTRACT

1 EGG

1 TABLESPOON SUGAR

NONSTICK COOKING SPRAY, FOR PREPARING THE WAFFLE MAKER

1. In a large bowl, whisk the flour, baking powder, baking soda, and salt. Add the milk, whisking until the ingredients are combined.

2. Whisk in the melted butter and vanilla until the batter has an even consistency.

3. In a small bowl, beat the egg until it is creamy and uniform in color. Add it to the batter and carefully fold it in. Sprinkle the sugar over the top and fold it in until the sugar is no longer visible. The batter should have very small lumps.

4. Cover the batter and refrigerate for at least 10 minutes.

5. Meanwhile, preheat your waffle maker, or, if you are using a stovetop waffle iron, heat it over medium heat.

(Continued)

6. Generously spray the top and bottom of the waffle maker or waffle iron with cooking spray. Using a ladle, drop in enough batter to cover about three-quarters of the iron's surface. If you are using a waffle maker, cook the waffles according to your waffle maker's instructions. If you are using a stovetop waffle iron, cook for about 90 seconds, flip, and cook for 60 seconds more.

7. Repeat with any remaining batter.

> **FOR A CROWD:** These waffles are sure to be a crowd pleaser, and the recipe can easily be scaled. If you are going through multiple rounds of waffle making, keep your first waffles as hot as your last by stashing the cooked waffles in a warm oven (200°F) while you work through the remainder of your batter.

For the Sous Chef:

Beat the egg as outlined in step 3 so your chef can focus on combining the other ingredients in steps 1 and 2.

FRENCH TOAST WITH PEACHES & HONEY

SERVES 2 | PREP TIME: 10 MINUTES | COOK TIME: 15 MINUTES

Cozy Comforts, Meatless Monday, Nut Free

Both of us grew up in families where French toast was a breakfast treat. We wanted to put our own spin on this memory by incorporating some of our favorite spring flavors— fresh peaches that have been slightly caramelized, and just a hint of honey in place of the conventional maple syrup.

1 TABLESPOON UNSALTED BUTTER, DIVIDED

1 EGG

½ CUP MILK

1 TEASPOON VANILLA EXTRACT

¾ TEASPOON GROUND CINNAMON

4 SLICES CHALLAH

1 PEACH, PEELED AND DICED

1 TABLESPOON PACKED LIGHT BROWN SUGAR

1½ TABLESPOONS HONEY

1. Heat a nonstick skillet over medium heat. Once the pan is hot, add 1½ teaspoons of butter to melt, tilting the pan to coat it fully.

2. In a shallow dish, whisk the egg, milk, vanilla, and cinnamon.

3. Dip each piece of bread into the milk mixture, making sure both sides are evenly coated.

4. Place the bread in the skillet and cook for 4 minutes before flipping and cooking for 3 minutes more.

5. In a separate skillet over medium heat, melt the remaining 1½ teaspoons of butter. Add the peaches and sprinkle the brown sugar over them. Cook, stirring occasionally, until the peaches are tender and the juices released are starting to reduce, about 6 minutes.

(Continued)

6. Place the French toast on the plate and top with the peach mixture. Drizzle with honey and serve.

> **SWAP IT OUT:** We love the fluffy texture of challah for French toast, but if isn't readily available, try brioche to achieve a similar consistency, or French bread cut at a long diagonal for a French toast with a chewier crust.

For the Sous Chef:

Begin cooking the peaches in step 5 while your chef starts the French toast in step 1. This will allow you to finish right around the same time!

GIANT CINNAMON ROLLS

SERVES 6 | PREP TIME: 2 HOURS | COOK TIME: 25 TO 30 MINUTES

Cozy Comforts, Meatless Monday, Nut Free

We might have saved the best breakfast recipe for last. These cinnamon rolls are larger than life—and their slightly cream-cheesy frosting is the perfect complement to the sweetness of the rolls and gooey filling!

FOR THE BUNS

1 ENVELOPE ACTIVE DRY YEAST (2¼ TEASPOONS)

½ CUP PLUS 2 TABLESPOONS WARM WATER

2¾ CUPS ALL-PURPOSE FLOUR, DIVIDED

¼ CUP SUGAR

½ TEASPOON SALT

4 TABLESPOONS UNSALTED BUTTER, MELTED, PLUS 4 TABLESPOONS AT ROOM TEMPERATURE, PLUS MORE FOR THE PAN

¼ CUP HEAVY (WHIPPING) CREAM, AT ROOM TEMPERATURE

1 EGG YOLK

½ TEASPOON VANILLA EXTRACT

½ CUP PACKED LIGHT BROWN SUGAR

1 TABLESPOON GROUND CINNAMON

FOR THE FROSTING

3½ TABLESPOONS UNSALTED BUTTER, AT ROOM TEMPERATURE

1 OUNCE CREAM CHEESE, AT ROOM TEMPERATURE

1 TABLESPOON MILK

¼ TEASPOON VANILLA EXTRACT

¾ CUP POWDERED SUGAR

⅛ TEASPOON SALT

TO MAKE THE ROLLS

1. In a medium bowl, sprinkle the yeast over the warm water. Let sit until the mixture starts to bubble, about 2 minutes.

2. In a large bowl, combine 2½ cups of flour, the sugar, and salt. Using a rubber spatula, stir the ingredients together. In a separate bowl, whisk the 4 tablespoons melted butter, heavy cream, egg yolk, and vanilla. Add the wet ingredients and the yeast to the dry ingredients. Using a rubber spatula, stir to form a rough dough.

3. Transfer the dough to the bowl of a stand mixer fitted with a dough hook. Knead on medium speed until the dough is soft, but pulls away easily from the sides of the bowl, 5 to 7 minutes. Cover the dough with plastic wrap and set aside for 1 hour.

(Continued)

4. While the dough is rising, prepare the filling. In a medium bowl, stir together the brown sugar and cinnamon, mixing until well combined. Set aside.

5. After an hour has elapsed, use the remaining ¼ cup of flour to dust your clean countertop. Slide the dough onto the floured surface and dust the top of the dough with more flour.

6. Using a rolling pin, gently roll the dough into a rectangle about 12 inches long by 16 inches wide, and about ⅓ inch thick. Spread the 4 tablespoons room-temperature butter evenly over the top of the dough.

7. Sprinkle the brown sugar and cinnamon filling over the entire buttered surface.

8. Starting with the edge of the dough closest to you, roll it away from you, being careful to ensure an even roll all the way to the end. Use a small amount of water to dampen the far edge of the dough and press it to the rolled log to seal it. Cut the log crosswise into six even slices.

9. Coat the inside of a square baking pan with butter. Place the rolls inside the pan, loosely cover, and let rise for 30 minutes. Meanwhile, preheat the oven to 350°F.

10. Bake the cinnamon rolls for 25 to 30 minutes, until they start to become golden and brown.

To make the frosting

1. While the rolls bake, in the (clean) bowl of the stand mixer fitted with the beater attachment, beat together the butter and cream cheese until creamy. Slowly mix in the milk and vanilla, followed by the powdered sugar and salt, mixing until the frosting is smooth.

2. Using a spatula, spread the frosting on top of the still-warm cinnamon buns.

> **PREP TIP:** If you don't have time to complete this recipe in one kitchen session, the dough can be made up to two days ahead. Let it rise in the refrigerator overnight to save an hour the next day!

For the Sous Chef:

While your chef starts the dough and is mixing the dry ingredients in step 2, you can mix the wet ingredients (also in step 2). Once the dough has risen, dust the countertop as outlined in step 5, finishing the dough, so your chef is ready to begin rolling right away. Finally, in step 8, finishing the dough, work together to roll the dough into a log.

Quick Bites

PROSCIUTTO & PEAR ARUGULA SALAD — 41

GRILLED CHICKEN & ROMAINE CAESAR — 42

CHOPPED KALE GREEK SALAD — 44

SIMPLE ASIAN SALAD WITH GINGER DRESSING — 45

SOUTHWEST CHICKEN & AVOCADO SALAD — 46

ROASTED ASIAN-STYLE BROCCOLI — 48

CRISPY GARLIC GREEN BEANS — 49

PARMESAN ROASTED ASPARAGUS — 50

ROASTED ROSEMARY POTATOES — 51

CHILI ROASTED SWEET POTATOES — 52

COCONUT STICKY RICE — 53

CORN BREAD MUFFINS — 55

CREAMY TOMATO SOUP — 56

WHITE BEAN HUMMUS — 57

SPINACH ARTICHOKE DIP — 58

TOMATO TART WITH BURRATA — 61

HOMEMADE PIZZA ROLLS — 62

BUFFALO CHICKEN MEATBALLS — 64

SPICY CHICKEN BITES — 65

TOMATO & BACON GRILLED CHEESE — 66

PROSCIUTTO & PEAR ARUGULA SALAD

SERVES 2 | PREP TIME: 15 MINUTES | COOK TIME: 10 MINUTES

Gluten Free, Weeknight

Salads can be so much more than chopped lettuce and cherry tomatoes. The key to a satisfying salad is incorporating a variety of textures in every bite. With crunchy prosciutto di Parma, crisp pears, and creamy goat cheese, this salad is a scrumptious light lunch. Pile on grilled chicken or shrimp for a quick and easy weeknight meal.

1 SLICE PROSCIUTTO DI PARMA

½ CUP PECAN HALVES

2 TABLESPOONS RED WINE VINEGAR

1 TABLESPOON EXTRA-VIRGIN OLIVE OIL

1 TABLESPOON WHOLE-GRAIN MUSTARD

1 TABLESPOON HONEY

3 CUPS ARUGULA

1 PEAR, SLICED

¼ CUP GOAT CHEESE, CRUMBLED

1. Preheat the oven to 350°F. Line a baking sheet with aluminum foil.

2. Arrange the prosciutto on the prepared baking sheet and carefully place the baking sheet into the oven. Bake for 5 minutes or until crispy. Let cool and then crumble the prosciutto.

3. Meanwhile, in a small cast-iron skillet over low heat, toast the pecans until fragrant.

4. In a small bowl, whisk the vinegar, olive oil, mustard, and honey.

5. Divide the arugula and top with sliced pear, toasted pecans, goat cheese crumbles, and crumbled prosciutto. Drizzle with dressing and toss to coat.

For the Sous Chef:

Preheat the oven, slice the pear, and make the dressing (step 4), while your chef is completing steps 2 and 3.

GRILLED CHICKEN & ROMAINE CAESAR

SERVES 2 | PREP TIME: 10 MINUTES | COOK TIME: 15 MINUTES

Gluten Free, Nut Free, Weeknight

This Caesar salad is anything but ordinary. Grilling the romaine lettuce leaves is a simple strategy that elevates this dish without much effort. Here, we outline the technique for making this dish on the stove so you can enjoy it year-round, but in summer we love to prepare the chicken and romaine outside on the grill. Pair this salad with glasses of white wine for a light and refreshing meal on a warm summer evening.

2 TABLESPOONS EXTRA-VIRGIN OLIVE OIL, DIVIDED

8 OUNCES THIN BONELESS, SKINLESS CHICKEN BREAST

SEA SALT

FRESHLY GROUND BLACK PEPPER

1 HEAD ROMAINE LETTUCE, TOPS AND BOTTOMS TRIMMED, HALVED LENGTHWISE

BOTTLED CAESAR DRESSING, FOR SERVING

2 TABLESPOONS PARMESAN FLAKES

1. In a medium cast-iron skillet over medium heat, heat 1 tablespoon of olive oil. Season the chicken with salt and pepper and place it in the skillet. Cook for 3 to 4 minutes per side, until the chicken is cooked through.

2. Heat a grill pan, or grill, to medium heat. Drizzle the remaining 1 tablespoon of olive oil over the lettuce. Place the lettuce in the pan and lightly grill for about 1 minute per side or until it is lightly golden.

3. Slice the chicken.

4. Divide the lettuce between two plates, add grilled chicken slices, drizzle with dressing, and sprinkle with Parmesan.

SWAP IT OUT: Swapping out store-bought dressing for homemade is a simple way to control the ingredients and pack even more flavor into every meal. To make Caesar dressing from scratch: In a blender or food processor, combine ¼ cup freshly squeezed lemon juice, 2 tablespoons mayonnaise, 2 teaspoons Dijon mustard, and 2 minced garlic cloves. Blend to combine. Season with salt and pepper and pulse in ¼ cup grated Parmesan cheese until smooth.

For the Sous Chef:

Prep the ingredients by washing and trimming the lettuce while the chef cooks the chicken in step 1. Once the chicken is done, move on to step 3.

CHOPPED KALE GREEK SALAD

SERVES 2 | PREP TIME: 15 MINUTES

Gluten Free, Meatless Monday, Nut Free, One Pot, Weeknight

You might think of chopped salads only as something you order at a restaurant, but in reality, they are one of the easiest dinners to throw together when you lack motivation or time—or both! Chop and slice whatever vegetables you have on hand and add them to a bed of chopped greens. Toss with a little EVOO and freshly squeezed lemon juice and you have a feel-good meal in minutes!

1 BUNCH KALE, MASSAGED AND CHOPPED (SEE INGREDIENT TIP)

½ ENGLISH CUCUMBER, CHOPPED

1 CUP CANNED CHICKPEAS, RINSED AND DRAINED

½ CUP CHERRY TOMATOES, HALVED

½ RED ONION, THINLY SLICED

¼ CUP KALAMATA OLIVES, PITTED AND HALVED

1/3 CUP CRUMBLED FETA CHEESE

1 TO 2 TEASPOONS FRESHLY SQUEEZED LEMON JUICE

1 TO 2 TABLESPOONS EXTRA-VIRGIN OLIVE OIL

FRESHLY GROUND BLACK PEPPER

1. In a large bowl, combine the kale, cucumber, chickpeas, tomatoes, red onion, olives, and feta cheese.

2. Drizzle with the lemon juice and olive oil, season with pepper, and gently toss to coat evenly.

> **INGREDIENT TIP:** Kale is a strong, bitter green that holds up well to being sautéed or braised in a hearty stew. But when using kale as a salad base, it is important to massage it to soften the texture and release natural sugars in the leaves, balancing the bitterness. Simply remove the ribs, drizzle with olive oil, add a pinch of sea salt, and gently knead the leaves with your fingers.

For the Sous Chef:

Prep the salad base by chopping and massaging the kale while the chef chops and slices the remaining ingredients.

SIMPLE ASIAN SALAD WITH GINGER DRESSING

SERVES 2 | PREP TIME: 20 MINUTES

Dairy Free, Meatless Monday, Weeknight

Filled with fresh greens, crisp veggies, and crunchy chow mein noodles, this salad is packed with flavor and texture. The dressing is bright and bold and is the perfect complement to the refreshing lettuce. Inspired by the starter salad at our favorite hibachi restaurant, this dressing also makes a wonderful marinade for salmon or dipping sauce for crudités. No matter how you use the dressing, it is sure to be the star.

¼ CUP CHOPPED ONION

¼ CUP PEANUT OIL

3 TABLESPOONS RICE VINEGAR

1 TABLESPOON WATER

1 TABLESPOON PEELED, GRATED FRESH GINGER

1 TABLESPOON CHOPPED CELERY

1 TABLESPOON KETCHUP

2 TEASPOONS SOY SAUCE

1¼ TEASPOONS SUGAR

1 TEASPOON FRESHLY SQUEEZED LEMON JUICE

¼ TEASPOON MINCED GARLIC

¼ TEASPOON SEA SALT

¼ TEASPOON FRESHLY GROUND BLACK PEPPER

3 CUPS CHOPPED ICEBERG LETTUCE

1 CUP SHREDDED RED CABBAGE

2 CARROTS, JULIENNED

¼ CUP SHELLED EDAMAME

¼ CUP CRUNCHY CHOW MEIN NOODLES

1. In a high-speed blender, combine the onion, peanut oil, vinegar, water, ginger, celery, ketchup, soy sauce, sugar, lemon juice, garlic, salt, and pepper. Blend until smooth.

2. In a large bowl, combine the lettuce, cabbage, carrots, edamame, and noodles.

3. Divide the salad between two bowls and drizzle with dressing.

For the Sous Chef:

Prep the ingredients by washing and chopping the lettuce and other vegetables.

SOUTHWEST CHICKEN & AVOCADO SALAD

SERVES 2 | PREP TIME: 15 MINUTES | COOK TIME: 10 MINUTES

Gluten Free, Nut Free, Weeknight

A hearty and flavorful main dish, this salad is in constant rotation in our house because it is as simple as it is delicious. Filled with fresh ingredients and packed with protein, it's easy to pull together for a light meal or meal prep for the week. We always have black beans, onions, bell peppers, avocados, and lemons on hand, so the only prep work is cooking the chicken, chopping the lettuce, and opening a few cans. We like adding this amped-up version of ranch dressing, but if you're in a time crunch or don't have a sous chef for the day, use plain ranch right out of the bottle.

1 TABLESPOON EXTRA-VIRGIN OLIVE OIL

2 BONELESS, SKINLESS CHICKEN BREASTS

1 TABLESPOON TACO SEASONING

3 CUPS CHOPPED ROMAINE LETTUCE

1 SMALL TOMATO, CHOPPED

½ CUP CORN, RINSED AND DRAINED

½ CUP BLACK BEANS, RINSED AND DRAINED

¼ RED ONION, CHOPPED

½ AVOCADO, SLICED

¼ CUP RANCH DRESSING

1 TEASPOON CHILI POWDER

1 TEASPOON GROUND CUMIN

SEA SALT

FRESHLY GROUND BLACK PEPPER

2 TABLESPOONS CHOPPED FRESH CILANTRO

½ LIME, CUT INTO WEDGES

1. In a medium cast-iron skillet over medium heat, heat the olive oil. Coat the chicken with the taco seasoning and add it to the skillet. Cook for 3 to 4 minutes per side or until the chicken is cooked through. Transfer to a cutting board and slice.

2. In a large bowl, combine the romaine, tomato, corn, black beans, and red onion.

3. In a small bowl, whisk the ranch dressing, chili powder, and cumin. Season with salt and pepper.

4. Divide the salad mixture between two shallow bowls and top with grilled chicken and avocado.

5. Drizzle with dressing and garnish with cilantro and lime wedges.

> **INGREDIENT TIP:** Forgot to pick up taco seasoning? Make your own by combining 4 teaspoons chili powder, 1 tablespoon ground cumin, 1 tablespoon paprika, 2 teaspoons onion powder, 1½ teaspoons garlic salt, and 1 teaspoon sea salt.

For the Sous Chef:

Prep the ingredients by washing and chopping the lettuce and other vegetables while the chef cooks the chicken in step 1. While the chef is putting together the salads in step 2, prepare the dressing in step 3.

ROASTED ASIAN-STYLE BROCCOLI

SERVES 2 | PREP TIME: 10 MINUTES | COOK TIME: 20 MINUTES

Dairy Free, Date Night, Meatless Monday, Nut Free

Roasted vegetables are really a "no-recipe recipe"—simply arrange the veggies on a sheet pan, pop the pan in the oven, and in about 20 minutes you'll have flavorful veggies sure to complement any meal. In this recipe, the sauce is the secret ingredient that elevates this dish from good to great. Sticky, sweet, and full of bold flavor, it can also be paired with asparagus, cauliflower, and an endless variety of other vegetables. Serve on the side or use it as a topping for your favorite grain bowl.

2 TABLESPOONS SOY SAUCE

2 TABLESPOONS BALSAMIC VINEGAR

1 TABLESPOON EXTRA-VIRGIN OLIVE OIL

1 TEASPOON MAPLE SYRUP

1 SMALL HEAD BROCCOLI, TRIMMED INTO FLORETS

RED PEPPER FLAKES, FOR GARNISH

SESAME SEEDS, FOR GARNISH

1. Preheat the oven to 425°F. Line a baking sheet with aluminum foil and set aside.

2. In a large bowl, whisk the soy sauce, vinegar, olive oil, and maple syrup.

3. Add the broccoli to the sauce and toss to coat evenly. Spread the broccoli in a single layer on the prepared baking sheet and roast for 20 minutes.

4. Remove from the oven and garnish with red pepper flakes and sesame seeds before serving.

> **INGREDIENT TIP:** The smaller and thinner the broccoli, the crispier it will get. For maximum crispness, halve the florets lengthwise.

For the Sous Chef:

Preheat the oven and trim the broccoli into florets.

CRISPY GARLIC GREEN BEANS

SERVES 2 | PREP TIME: 10 MINUTES | COOK TIME: 15 MINUTES

Dairy Free, Date Night, Meatless Monday, Nut Free

One of our go-to spots is Portland, Maine, where we travel at least once a year, and where Kenzie hosted her bachelorette weekend. There was one particular restaurant that was so good, she had to go back a few weeks later—with friends (and partners) in tow. All the girls could talk about was the "crispy green beans," so we ordered two servings. It seemed impossible the dish could live up to the hype but—proven wrong—we ordered a third plate for "dessert." This is our take on one of our Portland favorites.

2 TABLESPOONS SESAME OIL

4 GARLIC CLOVES, MINCED

1 (1-INCH) PIECE FRESH GINGER, PEELED AND MINCED

¼ TEASPOON RED PEPPER FLAKES

12 OUNCES FRENCH GREEN BEANS

2 TABLESPOONS SOY SAUCE

1 TABLESPOON RICE WINE VINEGAR

1 TEASPOON MAPLE SYRUP

1. In a medium cast-iron skillet over high heat, heat the sesame oil. Add the garlic, ginger, and red pepper flakes. Sauté for 30 seconds.

2. Add the green beans and toss to combine. Continue to cook, stirring, for about 5 minutes or until the beans begin to crisp on the ends.

3. In a small bowl, whisk the soy sauce, vinegar, and maple syrup.

4. Add the sauce to the skillet, reduce the heat to medium, and simmer the beans for 3 to 5 minutes or until the beans are crisp-tender and the sauce has reduced.

For the Sous Chef:

Prep the ingredients by mincing the garlic and ginger. While the chef is cooking, proceed to step 3 and make the sauce.

PARMESAN ROASTED ASPARAGUS

SERVES 2 | PREP TIME: 5 MINUTES | COOK TIME: 10 MINUTES

Date Night, Meatless Monday, Nut Free, One Pot

We have a motto in our house: Cheese makes everything better. This motto is rooted in the idea that salt and fat are important ingredients in any dish. Parmesan, in particular, is incredibly versatile and full of umami flavor. This sharp, salty, nutty cheese can be incorporated into a creamy pasta sauce, fried as a breading for your chicken cutlets, broiled on top of clams, sprinkled over French fries, and even enjoyed on its own. Here we use Parmesan to transform simple roasted asparagus into a savory masterpiece.

1 BUNCH FRESH ASPARAGUS, TRIMMED

1 TABLESPOON EXTRA-VIRGIN OLIVE OIL

1½ TEASPOONS UNSALTED BUTTER, MELTED

3 TABLESPOONS PANKO BREAD CRUMBS

4 TABLESPOONS FINELY GRATED PARMESAN CHEESE, DIVIDED

¼ TEASPOON GARLIC POWDER

¼ TEASPOON SEA SALT

¼ TEASPOON FRESHLY GROUND BLACK PEPPER

1. Preheat the oven to 425°F. Line a rimmed sheet pan with aluminum foil.

2. On the prepared sheet pan, combine the asparagus, olive oil, and melted butter and toss together to coat evenly. Spread the asparagus in a single layer.

3. Sprinkle with the bread crumbs, 3 tablespoons of Parmesan cheese, the garlic powder, salt, and pepper.

4. Roast for 8 to 10 minutes or until the asparagus is crisp-tender and the cheese is melted.

5. Remove from the oven and garnish with remaining 1 tablespoon of Parmesan before serving.

> **SWAP IT OUT:** If you don't have asparagus on hand, swap in broccoli, green beans, or any other vegetable you have.

For the Sous Chef:

Preheat the oven and trim the tough ends off the asparagus.

ROASTED ROSEMARY POTATOES

SERVES 2 | PREP TIME: 10 MINUTES | COOK TIME: 45 MINUTES

Dairy Free, Date Night, Gluten Free, Meatless Monday, Nut Free, One Pot

The perfect side dish for any occasion, roasted potatoes are just as yummy served with breakfast as they are with dinner. We love the classic combination of potatoes with rosemary, but you can vary the seasoning based on what's in your spice cabinet or what's growing in your garden! Pair these potatoes with our Tomato, Spinach & Goat Cheese Omelets (page 24) or Garlic & Herb Filet Mignon (page 84).

1 POUND SMALL RED POTATOES, HALVED

2 TABLESPOONS EXTRA-VIRGIN OLIVE OIL

2 TABLESPOONS FRESH ROSEMARY LEAVES, MINCED

½ TEASPOON SEA SALT

¼ TEASPOON FRESHLY GROUND BLACK PEPPER

1. Preheat the oven to 425°F. Line a rimmed sheet pan with aluminum foil.

2. On the prepared sheet pan, combine the potatoes, olive oil, rosemary, salt, and pepper and toss together to coat evenly. Spread the potatoes in a single layer.

3. Roast for 30 to 45 minutes, flipping halfway through the cooking time, until the potatoes are golden brown and crisp.

> **MIX IT UP:** Spice up these potatoes by adding 1 teaspoon paprika, sliced red bell pepper, and sliced onion along with the olive oil. This version makes the perfect brunch side dish.

For the Sous Chef:

Preheat the oven and prep the ingredients by rinsing and halving the potatoes.

CHILI ROASTED SWEET POTATOES

SERVES 2 | PREP TIME: 10 MINUTES | COOK TIME: 45 MINUTES

Dairy Free, Date Night, Gluten Free, Meatless Monday, Nut Free, One Pot

As you may have noticed, roasted vegetables make a frequent appearance on our dinner table. Roasted veggies can taste like a guilty pleasure, but they are good for you. After all, they are veggies and anything that gets you to eat more vegetables is a win in our book. When roasting vegetables, such as these Chili Roasted Sweet Potatoes, remember to use high heat, generally 425°F or higher, to ensure the vegetables cook quickly, brown on the outside, and stay tender on the inside.

2 SWEET POTATOES, PEELED AND CUBED

1 TABLESPOON EXTRA-VIRGIN OLIVE OIL

½ TEASPOON SEA SALT

¼ TEASPOON GROUND CUMIN

¼ TEASPOON CHILI POWDER

DASH CAYENNE PEPPER (OPTIONAL)

1. Preheat the oven to 425°F. Line a rimmed sheet pan with aluminum foil.

2. On the prepared sheet pan, combine the sweet potatoes, olive oil, salt, cumin, chili powder, and cayenne (if using) and toss together to coat evenly. Spread the potatoes in a single layer.

3. Roast for 35 to 45 minutes, flipping halfway through the cooking time, until the potatoes are golden brown and crisp.

> **MIX IT UP:** We love the contrast of sweet and spicy in this recipe, but if you want to keep with tradition and celebrate the sweetness of these potatoes, swap out the spices for 1 tablespoon honey and 1 teaspoon ground cinnamon.

For the Sous Chef:

Preheat the oven, peel and chop the sweet potatoes.

COCONUT STICKY RICE

SERVES 2 | PREP TIME: 45 MINUTES, PLUS OVERNIGHT TO SOAK |
COOK TIME: 1 HOUR 5 MINUTES

Cozy Comforts, Dairy Free, Date Night, Gluten Free, Nut Free

This side dish is based on a traditional Thai dessert (yes, dessert) that pairs warm sticky rice with chilled mango—but we first encountered coconut sticky rice at an Asian fusion restaurant that served the rice alongside a butternut squash curry. Since then, we have enjoyed this version as the perfect companion to many dishes, as well as in desserts. Sticky rice is traditionally soaked, then steam-cooked in a bamboo steamer. This saucepan method doesn't yield exactly the same results, but it works if your kitchen isn't outfitted with bamboo steamers. Note this requires an overnight soak, so plan ahead!

½ CUP DRY GLUTINOUS RICE

⅓ CUP PLUS 2 TABLESPOONS CANNED UNSWEETENED COCONUT MILK, WELL STIRRED, DIVIDED

2 TABLESPOONS PLUS 2 TEASPOONS SUGAR, DIVIDED

SEA SALT

SESAME SEEDS, TOASTED, FOR GARNISH

1. In a fine-mesh strainer, rinse the rice several times with cold water until the water runs clear.

2. In a large bowl, combine the rice with enough cold water to cover. Cover the bowl with a clean towel and let soak overnight.

3. Heat a large saucepan filled with water over medium heat until the water is simmering.

4. Drain the rice through a fine-mesh strainer and place the strainer above the water in the pot. The strainer should not touch the water.

5. Cover the pot with a lid and steam the rice for about 1 hour, or until it is tender and the water has evaporated. Add more water to the pot if needed.

6. While the rice cooks, heat a small saucepan over medium heat. Combine ⅓ cup of coconut milk, 2 tablespoons of sugar, and a pinch of salt in the pan. Bring to a boil, stirring until the sugar is dissolved.

(Continued)

7. Remove the pan from the heat; cover with aluminum foil to keep it warm.

8. In another large bowl, combine the cooked rice and coconut milk mixture, stirring until evenly mixed. Cover the bowl and let the rice stand for about 30 minutes or until all the liquid is absorbed.

9. While the rice stands, heat a small saucepan over medium-high heat. Combine the remaining 2 tablespoons of coconut milk and 2 teaspoons of sugar. Bring the mixture to a boil and cook for 1 minute. Transfer the mixture to a small bowl and refrigerate until it thickens slightly.

10. To serve, top the rice with the chilled coconut milk mixture and garnish with sesame seeds.

> **INGREDIENT TIP:** Unlike plain sticky rice, coconut sticky rice has enough moisture and oil in it that it keeps for 24 hours in a covered container in the refrigerator without drying out. Use the microwave to reheat it the next day.

For the Sous Chef:

Prep the rice in steps 1 and 2. The following day, complete step 3 while your chef drains the rice. Then proceed to step 9 to prep the remaining coconut milk mixture.

CORN BREAD MUFFINS

MAKES 12 muffins | PREP TIME: 10 MINUTES | COOK TIME: 20 MINUTES

Cozy Comforts, Date Night, Meatless Monday, Nut Free

One of our favorite tricks when cooking for two is to use a recipe that's traditionally made for a crowd, but package it in a way that is easy to portion for two. This recipe will easily fill a loaf pan, but we use a muffin tin instead. We use this technique for a variety of dishes, including breakfast frittatas, mini meatloaves, and Mini Cheesecakes (page 114).

1 CUP ALL-PURPOSE FLOUR

1 CUP CORNMEAL

⅓ CUP SUGAR

2 TEASPOONS BAKING POWDER

½ TEASPOON SEA SALT

1 CUP WHOLE MILK

1 EGG, BEATEN

¼ CUP VEGETABLE OIL

1. Preheat the oven to 400°F. Line a muffin tin with paper liners and set aside.

2. In a large bowl, stir together the flour, cornmeal, sugar, baking powder, and salt. Add the milk, egg, and vegetable oil and stir to combine.

3. Spoon the batter into the prepared muffin cups. Bake for 15 to 20 minutes or until the muffins are golden brown and a toothpick inserted into the center of one comes out clean.

For the Sous Chef:

Complete steps 1 and 2 by preheating the oven and lining the muffin tin while the chef prepares the batter. Once the batter is complete, help the chef spoon the batter into the muffin cups.

CREAMY TOMATO SOUP

SERVES 2 | PREP TIME: 5 MINUTES | COOK TIME: 1 HOUR

Cozy Comforts, Gluten Free, Meatless Monday, Nut Free, One Pot

Middle of winter or dead of summer, tomato soup can cure just about any woe and make you feel all warm and fuzzy inside. It is the ultimate cure when you are craving something extra comforting. We love the velvety smooth texture that the cream provides, but if you prefer a more rustic soup, omit it and serve after blending to your desired consistency. Serve alone or alongside our Tomato & Bacon Grilled Cheese (page 66).

1 TABLESPOON UNSALTED BUTTER

½ SMALL ONION, CHOPPED

1 GARLIC CLOVE, MINCED

1 TABLESPOON TOMATO PASTE

2 CUPS WATER

1 (14-OUNCE) CAN CRUSHED TOMATOES

¼ TEASPOON SUGAR

SEA SALT

FRESHLY GROUND BLACK PEPPER

2 TABLESPOONS HEAVY (WHIPPING) CREAM

FRESH BASIL, FOR GARNISH

RED PEPPER FLAKES, FOR GARNISH

EXTRA-VIRGIN OLIVE OIL, FOR GARNISH

1. In a large pot over medium-high heat, melt the butter. Add the onion and garlic and sauté for about 8 minutes, until translucent.

2. Stir in the tomato paste and continue cooking for about 6 minutes, stirring frequently. Add the water, tomatoes, and sugar. Bring to a boil.

3. Reduce the heat to medium-low and cook for 30 minutes. Season the soup with salt and pepper.

4. Remove from the heat and blend, using an immersion blender, until smooth.

5. Return the pot to the heat, stir in the heavy cream, and simmer for 10 minutes.

6. Divide the soup between two bowls and garnish with basil, red pepper flakes, and olive oil.

For the Sous Chef:

Prep the ingredients by peeling and chopping the onion and garlic. Then proceed to opening the can of tomatoes and measuring the other ingredients.

WHITE BEAN HUMMUS

MAKES 1½ CUPS | PREP TIME: 10 MINUTES

Dairy Free, Gluten Free, Meatless Monday, Nut Free, One Pot

We are firm believers in homemade hummus. Not to say we've never purchased a tub for convenience when entertaining or traveling, but there is no comparison to the flavor you are able to build with this homemade version. Traditionally, hummus is prepared with chickpeas, but cannellini beans are a great, healthy alternative that create an ultra-smooth, creamy texture. Our thick hummus is full of rich flavors from the fruity olive oil, silky tahini, and bright lemon. Pair as a dip with veggies or crackers, or sub for mayonnaise on your favorite sandwich or even in chicken salad.

1 (15-OUNCE) CAN CANNELLINI BEANS, DRAINED AND RINSED

2 TABLESPOONS EXTRA-VIRGIN OLIVE OIL

1 TABLESPOON TAHINI

JUICE OF 1 LEMON

1 GARLIC CLOVE, MINCED

SEA SALT

In a high-speed blender, combine the cannellini beans, olive oil, tahini, lemon juice, garlic, and a pinch of salt. Blend until smooth.

> **MIX IT UP:** Create a bolder flavor profile by adding 3 or 4 roasted garlic cloves, ¼ teaspoon ground cumin, and a pinch of smoked paprika. Another option is to add chopped fresh herbs, such as chives or basil.

For the Sous Chef:

Prep the ingredients by draining and rinsing the beans, prep any veggies or crackers for dipping.

SPINACH ARTICHOKE DIP

SERVES 6 TO 8 | PREP TIME: 10 MINUTES | COOK TIME: 20 MINUTES

Cozy Comforts, Gluten Free, Meatless Monday, Nut Free

Whether served hot or cold, spinach dip is always welcome at any get-together. That is why we consider it a staple recipe that every newlywed should know how to make. If you like your spinach dip hot and melty, this recipe is sure to be your new favorite. Perfect for when you're hosting game night or if you're headed to a housewarming, it's easy to pull together in advance and heat up when guests are getting hungry. Serve with veggies, tortilla chips, or crackers, and enjoy!

NONSTICK COOKING SPRAY, FOR PREPARING THE BAKING DISH

8 OUNCES CREAM CHEESE, AT ROOM TEMPERATURE

1 CUP SHREDDED MOZZARELLA CHEESE

⅔ CUP SHREDDED PARMESAN CHEESE

1 OUNCE PLAIN GREEK YOGURT

1 (14-OUNCE) CAN ARTICHOKE HEARTS, DRAINED AND QUARTERED

6 OUNCES FROZEN SPINACH, THAWED, DRAINED, AND CHOPPED

2 GARLIC CLOVES, MINCED

¼ TEASPOON SEA SALT

¼ TEASPOON FRESHLY GROUND BLACK PEPPER

1. Preheat the oven to 350°F. Coat a baking dish with cooking spray and set aside.

2. In a large bowl, stir together the cream cheese, mozzarella cheese, Parmesan cheese, and yogurt until well combined. Fold in the artichoke hearts, spinach, and garlic. Season with salt and pepper.

3. Spread the mixture evenly into the prepared baking dish.

4. Bake for about 20 minutes or until the cheese is melted and the top is golden brown.

> **KITCHEN HACK:** Prep this recipe in advance and keep it in the freezer for last-minute guests or when you need to bring an appetizer to a friend's house. Spread the mixture in an aluminum pan, cover, and freeze. It will store well for up to three months. To heat, bake at 350°F for 40 minutes or until melty and warmed through.

For the Sous Chef:

Prep the ingredients by ensuring the artichoke hearts and spinach are drained and chopped.

TOMATO TART WITH BURRATA

SERVES 2 | PREP TIME: 5 MINUTES | COOK TIME: 20 MINUTES

Cozy Comforts, Meatless Monday, One Pot, Weeknight

With its delicious mozzarella-esque exterior and dreamy, creamy center, burrata classes up any dish. We've combined it with the bright taste of roasted tomatoes on this tart—a savory, flavorful, and beautiful snack that is much simpler than you might think.

1 SHEET FROZEN PUFF
PASTRY, THAWED

1 TOMATO, THINLY SLICED

¼ CUP 5-INGREDIENT PESTO
(PAGE 185)

1 TABLESPOON EXTRA-VIRGIN
OLIVE OIL

SEA SALT

FRESHLY GROUND
BLACK PEPPER

1 (4-OUNCE) PIECE BURRATA

8 FRESH BASIL LEAVES

1. Preheat the oven to 400°F. Line a baking sheet with parchment paper and set aside.

2. Line a plate with a paper towel and arrange the tomato slices in a single layer. Place another paper towel on top to absorb liquid from both sides.

3. Unfold the puff pastry and lay it on the prepared baking sheet. Spread the pesto evenly atop the puff pastry, leaving a small border along the edges. Top with the tomato slices, making sure that none of the pieces overlap. Lightly drizzle the olive oil over the tart and season with salt and pepper.

4. Bake for 20 minutes, or until the puff pastry rises and is golden brown along the edges.

5. Remove the tart from the oven. Cut the burrata into several pieces and spread over the tart. Arrange the basil leaves on top and serve.

For the Sous Chef:

Prep the ingredients by slicing and draining the tomato in step 2.
While the chef removes the tart from the oven, cut up the burrata.

HOMEMADE PIZZA ROLLS

MAKES 12 ROLLS | PREP TIME: 15 MINUTES | COOK TIME: 10 MINUTES

Cozy Comforts, Nut Free

Pinwheel appetizers and snacks are trending because these tasty, bite-size treats come together in a snap. This version is a twist on a childhood favorite. Stuffed with pepperoni, mozzarella cheese, and pizza sauce, you get the full pizza experience in one little bite. Once you have mastered this recipe, mix things up and try other flavor combinations—like barbecue chicken, pesto and cheese, or buffalo cauliflower. You can even turn this into a sweet treat by swapping out the pepperoni, cheese, and sauce for Chocolate-Hazelnut Spread (page 183). Whip up a few of these pinwheel appetizers for your next party, or as a quick and easy snack!

ALL-PURPOSE FLOUR, FOR DUSTING

1 POUND PREMADE PIZZA DOUGH

1 CUP PIZZA SAUCE

2 CUPS SHREDDED MOZZARELLA CHEESE

1 CUP SLICED PEPPERONI, CHOPPED

2 TABLESPOONS UNSALTED BUTTER, MELTED

½ TEASPOON GARLIC POWDER

½ TEASPOON ITALIAN SEASONING

¼ CUP GRATED PARMESAN CHEESE

1. Preheat the oven to 400°F. Line a baking sheet with parchment paper and set aside.

2. Lightly flour a clean work surface and roll out the pizza dough into a rectangle, about 10 by 14 inches. Spread the pizza sauce across the top of the dough and top with the cheese and pepperoni.

3. In a small bowl, whisk the melted butter, garlic powder, and Italian seasoning.

4. Starting with the long end, tightly roll up the dough. Slice the roll crosswise into 1-inch pieces. Arrange the rolls in a single layer on the prepared baking sheet. Brush the butter mixture over the rolls.

5. Bake for 10 minutes or until golden brown. Remove from the oven and garnish with Parmesan cheese.

FOR A CROWD: These homemade pizza rolls are not only a delicious snack for two, but also the perfect appetizer for a crowd. If you are hosting a party, double the recipe and divide the dough into two rectangles so it is easier to work with.

For the Sous Chef:

Preheat the oven in step 1 and then proceed to step 3 while the chef prepares the dough.

BUFFALO CHICKEN MEATBALLS

SERVES 2 | PREP TIME: 10 MINUTES | COOK TIME: 15 MINUTES

Cozy Comforts, Nut Free, Weeknight

In our house, you can put buffalo sauce on just about anything and it is sure to be a hit. From classic buffalo chicken wings to buffalo cauliflower bites, you really can't go wrong. Buffalo chicken meatballs are a twist on everyone's go-to. With celery and carrot throughout the meatball, every bite is filled with the buffalo chicken flavors we love. They make great little snacks on game day, but you can also turn them into a meatball sub or serve them with steamed rice.

8 OUNCES GROUND CHICKEN

1 CELERY STALK, MINCED

½ CARROT, MINCED

1 EGG

2 TABLESPOONS CRUMBLED BLUE CHEESE

2 TABLESPOONS BUffALO SAUCE

2 TABLESPOONS BREAD CRUMBS

1. Preheat the oven to 400°F. Line a baking sheet with parchment paper and set aside.

2. In a large bowl, mix together the chicken, celery, carrot, egg, blue cheese, buffalo sauce, and bread crumbs. Shape the mixture into 1½-inch meatballs.

3. Arrange the meatballs in a single layer on the prepared baking sheet. Roast for about 15 minutes or until golden brown and cooked through.

For the Sous Chef:

Preheat the oven and prep the ingredients by mincing the veggies.

SPICY CHICKEN BITES

SERVES 2 | PREP TIME: 30 MINUTES | COOK TIME: 10 TO 15 MINUTES

Cozy Comforts, Dairy Free, Nut Free

Nothing says "quick bite" like chicken nuggets, but these aren't the frozen nuggets from your youth. We have packed these fancy little chicken bites with flavor and dialed up the heat. If you are looking for a quick and easy snack, these fill the bill. Serve with toothpicks and your favorite condiments. You can also make them over the weekend and keep them in the fridge to add some protein to your favorite salad. We think they are a great substitute for the grilled chicken in our Southwest Chicken & Avocado Salad (page 46).

1 BONELESS, SKINLESS CHICKEN BREAST, CUBED

¼ CUP EXTRA-VIRGIN OLIVE OIL

2 GARLIC CLOVES, MINCED

¼ CUP BREAD CRUMBS

¼ TEASPOON PAPRIKA

DASH CAYENNE PEPPER

SEA SALT

FRESHLY GROUND BLACK PEPPER

1. In a large bowl, combine the chicken, olive oil, and garlic and toss to coat evenly. Cover and let marinate for 20 minutes.

2. Preheat the oven to 475°F. Line a baking sheet with aluminum foil and set aside.

3. In another large bowl, stir together the bread crumbs, paprika, and cayenne. Season with salt and pepper. Add the chicken and toss to coat.

4. Spread the chicken in a single layer on the prepared baking sheet and bake for 10 to 15 minutes, flipping halfway through the cooking time, until golden brown and crisp.

For the Sous Chef:

After the chicken has marinated, preheat the oven and line the baking sheet with aluminum foil.

TOMATO & BACON GRILLED CHEESE

SERVES 2 | PREP TIME: 5 MINUTES | COOK TIME: 15 MINUTES

Cozy Comforts, Nut Free, Weeknight

While anyone can make a grilled cheese, there's an art to achieving perfectly melted cheese and golden brown toasted bread. And when you then stuff it with bright fresh tomatoes and crisp bacon, it's on a another level—and a new go-to snack on summer afternoons when tomatoes are in season. You can also pair this sandwich with a bowl of soup on a chilly day.

4 BACON SLICES

2 TABLESPOONS UNSALTED BUTTER

4 SOURDOUGH BREAD SLICES

⅓ CUP GRATED GRUYÈRE CHEESE

4 TOMATO SLICES

1. Heat a large skillet over medium-high heat. Add the bacon and cook, turning every 2 to 3 minutes, until fully crispy, about 10 minutes. Drain and set the bacon aside.

2. Return the skillet to medium heat. Spread butter onto one side of each slice of bread. Place two slices, buttered-side down, into the skillet.

3. Divide half of the Gruyère cheese evenly over the two slices of bread. Top each slice of bread with 2 tomato slices, 2 bacon slices, and the remaining cheese, dividing it evenly. Cover each with the remaining bread slices, buttered-side out.

4. Cook each sandwich until it is golden and toasted on the bottom, 4 to 5 minutes. Flip and cook for 2 to 3 minutes on the other side.

For the Sous Chef:

Prep the ingredients by grating the cheese and slicing the tomato. While the chef cooks the bacon, butter the bread in step 2.

Dinner Dates

PROSCIUTTO-WRAPPED CHICKEN	**68**
EASY CHICKEN & SHIITAKE RAMEN	**69**
CHICKEN & CHICKPEA TIKKA MASALA	**70**
THAI RED CURRY CHICKEN	**72**
CREAMY SUN-DRIED TOMATO CHICKEN PASTA	**74**
CARNITAS TACOS WITH PICKLED RED ONION & SLAW	**76**
CLASSIC BEEF STEW	**78**
CARBONARA RISOTTO	**80**
CREAMY TOMATO & SAUSAGE RIGATONI	**82**
GARLIC & HERB FILET MIGNON	**84**
FALAFEL GYROS WITH TZATZIKI	**85**
SUMMER VEGGIE ORECCHIETTE & PESTO	**87**
CAULIFLOWER & RICOTTA PIZZA	**89**
CACIO E PEPE	**91**
LOAF PAN EGGPLANT LASAGNA	**93**
HONEY SRIRACHA-GLAZED SALMON	**95**
MUSSELS IN WHITE WINE & GARLIC WITH CRUSTY BREAD	**96**
COD & VEGETABLES EN PAPILLOTE	**98**
SHRIMP PAD THAI	**100**
BAKED LOBSTER MACARONI & CHEESE	**102**

PROSCIUTTO-WRAPPED CHICKEN

SERVES 2 | PREP TIME: 15 MINUTES | COOK TIME: 30 MINUTES

Cozy Comforts, Date Night, Gluten Free, Nut Free

This recipe sounds (and looks) more complicated than it really is. The rich, aromatic butter sauce is a perfect complement to the salty prosciutto that crisps up on the outside of the chicken.

2 BONELESS, SKINLESS CHICKEN BREASTS

4 SLICES PROSCIUTTO DI PARMA

2 TABLESPOONS MELTED UNSALTED BUTTER, DIVIDED

SEA SALT

FRESHLY GROUND BLACK PEPPER

½ GARLIC CLOVE, MINCED

1 TEASPOON ITALIAN SEASONING

⅛ TEASPOON RED PEPPER FLAKES

¼ CUP DRY WHITE WINE

2 LEMON WEDGES

1. Preheat the oven to 450°F. Wrap each chicken breast with two slices of prosciutto, covering as much of the surface area as possible. Place the chicken breasts in a small baking dish and cover with 1 tablespoon of melted butter. Season with salt and pepper.

2. Bake the chicken for 18 minutes or until the thickest part reaches an internal temperature of 165°F. Remove from the oven, tent with foil, and let rest for 5 minutes.

3. Place the remaining 1 tablespoon of butter in a small pan over medium-low heat. Add the garlic, Italian seasoning, and red pepper flakes. Sauté for 5 minutes. Add the white wine and simmer for 5 minutes more.

4. Spoon the herb–wine sauce over the chicken and serve with lemon wedges for squeezing.

For the Sous Chef:

Preheat the oven, melt the butter, and mince the garlic. While the chef is tending to the chicken, start the sauce in step 3.

EASY CHICKEN & SHIITAKE RAMEN

SERVES 2 | PREP TIME: 10 MINUTES | COOK TIME: 10 MINUTES

Cozy Comforts, One Pot, Weeknight

There are few things that comfort Kenzie as much as a bowl of this ramen when she is sick. In fact, Julien knows to whip it up the second she starts sniffling This recipe may use the same dried ramen noodles you know and love from the package, but the flavorful broth is made from fresh ingredients instead of the sodium-filled packet. While this dish may not be authentic ramen, we find our homemade version just as flavorful and comforting.

1 TABLESPOON SESAME OIL

4 GARLIC CLOVES, MINCED

1 TABLESPOON PEELED AND MINCED FRESH GINGER

5 CUPS CHICKEN STOCK

1 CUP WATER

3 TABLESPOONS SOY SAUCE

2 TABLESPOONS RICE VINEGAR

1 TEASPOON FISH SAUCE

1 TEASPOON CHILI GARLIC SAUCE

1 CUP SHREDDED COOKED CHICKEN

½ CUP STEMMED AND SLICED SHIITAKE MUSHROOMS

SEA SALT

1 (7-OUNCE) PACKET RAMEN NOODLES

SESAME SEEDS, FOR GARNISH

1. In a large pot over high heat, heat the sesame oil. Add the garlic and ginger and sauté for 1 minute.

2. Add the chicken stock, water, soy sauce, vinegar, fish sauce, chili garlic sauce, chicken, scallions, and mushrooms to the pot. Season with salt and bring to a boil. Place the noodles in the soup mixture and cook for 2 minutes or until soft.

3. Divide between two bowls and garnish with sesame seeds.

For the Sous Chef:

Prep the ingredients by mincing the garlic and ginger, chopping the scallions, and slicing the mushrooms.

CHICKEN & CHICKPEA TIKKA MASALA

SERVES 2 | PREP TIME: 15 MINUTES | COOK TIME: 30 MINUTES

Nut Free

Julien loves the bold flavors and strong spices of Indian food, so when Kenzie first made chicken tikka masala at home, it was a surprise for Julien. While we can't remember exactly what we were celebrating, we do remember how the fragrant spices filled the kitchen, and how delicious the meal was. Kenzie has continued to modify her original recipe, and Julien taste-tested every version until we landed on this one. We hope you make as many memories as we have cooking it together.

2 TABLESPOONS MASALA PASTE, DIVIDED

½ CUP PLAIN GREEK YOGURT

8 OUNCES BONELESS, SKINLESS CHICKEN BREAST, DICED

¾ CUP CANNED CHICKPEAS, RINSED AND DRAINED

¾ CUP FULL-FAT COCONUT MILK

½ CUP TOMATO PURÉE

SEA SALT

COOKED BASMATI RICE, FOR SERVING (OPTIONAL)

FRESH CILANTRO, FOR GARNISH (OPTIONAL)

1. In a medium bowl, stir together 1½ teaspoons of masala paste and the yogurt. Add the chicken and toss to coat evenly. Cover the bowl with plastic wrap or aluminum foil and refrigerate to marinate for 10 to 15 minutes.

2. Heat a large cast-iron skillet over medium-high heat. Add the remaining 1½ tablespoons of masala paste and cook for 2 to 3 minutes, stirring frequently.

3. Add the chicken, ensuring that all the yogurt mixture from the bowl is added to the skillet, and cook for 5 to 8 minutes, stirring occasionally, until cooked through.

4. Stir in the chickpeas, coconut milk, and tomato purée. Simmer for 15 minutes. Season with salt and let stand for about 5 minutes, until the sauce begins to thicken. Serve with rice, garnished with cilantro (if using).

> **PREP TIP:** Masala paste is available at many grocery stores, but if you prefer to make your own, visit Kenzie's website (kenzieswanhart.com) for a recipe made from vegetables, herbs, and spices.

For the Sous Chef:

Prep the ingredients by dicing the chicken, and draining and rinsing the chickpeas. Once the chicken is almost finished marinating in step 1, get started on step 2.

THAI RED CURRY CHICKEN

SERVES 2 | PREP TIME: 15 MINUTES | COOK TIME: 15 MINUTES

Cozy Comforts, Dairy Free, Gluten Free, Nut Free, One Pot, Weeknight

Like so many of the other takeout-inspired dishes throughout this book, this recipe comes together in about 30 minutes—start to finish. That means you will have dinner on the table in less time than it would take to get food delivered. Not to mention, this one-pot dish brings together simple ingredients bursting with flavor—with way less guilt than your favorite takeout place. Just don't forget to cook some rice to serve on the side!

1 TABLESPOON VEGETABLE OIL

½ BUNCH SCALLIONS, THINLY SLICED

2 GARLIC CLOVES, MINCED

1 JALAPEÑO PEPPER, SEEDED AND DICED

1 CUP UNSWEETENED CANNED COCONUT MILK

1 TABLESPOON RED CURRY PASTE

1 TABLESPOON FISH SAUCE

1 TABLESPOON PACKED DARK BROWN SUGAR

1 RED BELL PEPPER, CUT INTO THIN STRIPS

1 POUND BONELESS, SKINLESS CHICKEN BREAST, DICED INTO 1-INCH CUBES

JUICE OF ½ LIME

2 TABLESPOONS CHOPPED FRESH CILANTRO

COOKED JASMINE RICE, FOR SERVING

1. In a large nonstick pan over medium-low heat, heat the vegetable oil. Add the scallions, garlic, and jalapeño and cook for 3 minutes or until soft.

2. Whisk in the coconut milk, red curry paste, fish sauce, and brown sugar until all the ingredients are combined. Bring the sauce to a low boil and simmer for 3 to 4 minutes, until thickened.

3. Carefully add the red bell pepper and chicken to the sauce and simmer for about 5 minutes, stirring often, until the pepper is tender and chicken is cooked through.

4. Stir in the lime juice and cilantro. Serve with the jasmine rice.

> **SWAP IT OUT:** Make this recipe "Meatless Monday"—approved by replacing the chicken with more vegetables. Sliced carrots, yellow and orange bell pepper, and cauliflower all make great additions!

For the Sous Chef:

Prep the ingredients by slicing the scallions, mincing the garlic, seeding and dicing the jalapeño, cutting the red bell pepper, dicing the chicken, and chopping the cilantro.

CREAMY SUN-DRIED TOMATO CHICKEN PASTA

SERVES 2 | PREP TIME: 5 MINUTES | COOK TIME: 15 MINUTES

Cozy Comforts, Nut Free, Weeknight

We are big proponents of simple ingredients coming together to make a delicious meal. This creamy pasta is a quick and easy meal that is sure to make it into your weeknight routine. We love the silky, rich cream sauce that pulls together sharp, salty Parmesan cheese and smooth mozzarella, bright and acidic sun-dried tomatoes, and the gentle heat of the garlic with tender, sliced chicken.

1½ CUPS DRY PENNE PASTA

2 TEASPOONS EXTRA-VIRGIN OLIVE OIL, DIVIDED

1 BONELESS, SKINLESS CHICKEN BREAST

SEA SALT

FRESHLY GROUND BLACK PEPPER

1 GARLIC CLOVE, MINCED

¼ CUP DRAINED OIL-PACKED SUN-DRIED TOMATOES

½ CUP HEAVY (WHIPPING) CREAM

½ CUP GRATED PARMESAN CHEESE

1. Bring a large pot of water to a boil over high heat. Cook the penne pasta according to the package directions until al dente. Drain.

2. In a large skillet over medium-low heat, heat 1 teaspoon of olive oil. Place the chicken breast in the skillet and season with salt and pepper. Cook for 5 minutes, flip, and cook for 5 more minutes or until the thickest part of the chicken breast has reached an internal temperature of 165°F on an instant-read thermometer. Remove the chicken, set it aside, and return the skillet to the stove.

3. Increase the heat to medium and add the remaining 1 teaspoon of olive oil to the skillet along with the garlic and sun-dried tomatoes. Sauté for 30 seconds.

4. Turn the heat to medium-high and add the heavy cream and Parmesan cheese. Cook for 3 minutes, reducing the heat to low once the sauce begins to simmer.

5. Slice the cooked chicken and add it and the pasta to the skillet, using tongs to distribute the chicken and tomatoes evenly and fully coat the pasta with the sauce.

PREP TIP: If you're a weekend meal prep aficionado, cook the chicken ahead of time so you can focus your efforts on the pasta and sauce. When you're ready to eat, heat it up and slice it just like you would if you cooked everything together.

For the Sous Chef:

Prep the ingredients by mincing the garlic. Boil the water and cook the pasta in step 1 while the chef gets started on step 2.

CARNITAS TACOS WITH PICKLED RED ONION & SLAW

SERVES 2 | PREP TIME: 15 MINUTES | COOK TIME: 8 HOURS

Cozy Comforts, Dairy Free, Date Night, Gluten Free, Nut Free

One of the first meals we cooked together was tacos—specifically, we made ground beef tacos using one of those kits in a box. While we have to admit those are still an occasional guilty pleasure, we do "Taco Tuesday" a bit differently these days. This recipe combines soft corn tortillas, slow-cooked pork carnitas, homemade pickled red onions, and cool, crunchy slaw. Our recipe serves two, but we highly recommend doubling the pork so you have leftovers for lunch or a night later in the week. This is the one recipe Julien is known to enjoy as leftovers on almost anything—including salads!

- 2 POUNDS BONELESS PORK SHOULDER
- ½ WHITE ONION, DICED
- JUICE OF ½ ORANGE
- JUICE OF ½ LIME
- ¼ CUP COLA
- 1 TEASPOON DRIED OREGANO
- 1 TEASPOON GROUND CUMIN
- 2 GARLIC CLOVES, MINCED

- SEA SALT
- FRESHLY GROUND BLACK PEPPER
- 1 CUP WARM WATER
- ½ CUP PLUS 1 TABLESPOON APPLE CIDER VINEGAR, DIVIDED
- 1 TABLESPOON SUGAR
- 1 RED ONION, THINLY SLICED
- 1 CUP BAGGED COLESLAW MIX

- 1 TEASPOON DIJON MUSTARD
- 2 TABLESPOONS OLIVE OIL
- 4 SMALL CORN TORTILLAS
- DICED AVOCADO, FOR SERVING (OPTIONAL)
- CRUMBLED QUESO FRESCO, FOR SERVING (OPTIONAL)
- FRESH CILANTRO, FOR GARNISH (OPTIONAL)

1. In a multi-cooker, combine the pork, onion, orange juice, lime juice, cola, oregano, cumin, garlic, and a few pinches each of salt and pepper. Cover the cooker and slow cook for 8 hours on low or 5 hours on high. When the pork is done, remove it from the multi-cooker, shred it using two forks, and set aside.

2. In a medium bowl, whisk together the water, ½ cup of vinegar, the sugar, and 1½ teaspoons of salt until the sugar and salt are fully dissolved. Add the red onion slices and toss to ensure they are fully coated. Let sit to pickle for at least 1 hour before eating.

3. In a separate bowl, combine the coleslaw mix, the remaining 1 tablespoon of vinegar, mustard, and olive oil. Season with salt and pepper. Using tongs or two spoons, gently toss to make sure all the coleslaw mix is coated.

4. Assemble the tacos by spooning the carnitas on top of the tortillas. Top with avocado and queso fresco, as desired, and garnish with cilantro (if using).

> **PREP TIP:** Pickled red onions are a delicious topping on these tacos—but the onions do need a little time to absorb the pickling mixture. Keep pickled onions in a jar, and they will stay fresh and ready to use from the refrigerator for up to one month.

For the Sous Chef:

While the chef is preparing the carnitas in step 1, make the pickled red onion in step 2 and the slaw in step 3. You can also pre-make both of these, refrigerate them, and have everything ready to go when you are ready to assemble your tacos.

CLASSIC BEEF STEW

SERVES 2 | PREP TIME: 15 MINUTES | COOK TIME: 2 HOURS, 15 MINUTES

Cozy Comforts, Dairy Free, Date Night, Nut Free, One Pot

Beef stew is a classic. In fact, it's a global comfort-food staple—from traditional French beef bourguignon to Hungarian goulash. Regardless of the specific ingredients, all versions of this classic stew include meat, veggies, and a gravy, cooked low and slow to tenderize the meat and build rich flavors. We developed this recipe by combining the ingredients in each of our family's recipes. Start here, and then swap ingredients in and out until you create your own recipe to pass down.

2 TEASPOONS EXTRA-VIRGIN OLIVE OIL

8 OUNCES STEW BEEF, CUT INTO 1-INCH CUBES

SEA SALT

FRESHLY GROUND BLACK PEPPER

½ WHITE ONION, DICED

1 GARLIC CLOVE, MINCED

1 CARROT, DICED

1 PARSNIP, DICED

½ CELERY STALK, DICED

1 TABLESPOON ALL-PURPOSE FLOUR

½ CUP BEEF STOCK

⅓ CUP DRY RED WINE (CABERNET SAUVIGNON OR PINOT NOIR)

1 TABLESPOON TOMATO PASTE

½ TEASPOON WORCESTERSHIRE SAUCE

1 DRIED BAY LEAF

1 POTATO, PEELED AND DICED

1. In a large, heavy-bottomed pot over high heat, heat the olive oil until it begins to smoke.

2. Add the stew beef to the pot, season with salt and pepper, and sear it on all sides until browned, about 5 minutes total. Remove the beef and set aside.

3. Turn the heat to medium-high and add the onion and garlic. Cook for 2 minutes or until the onion starts to become translucent. Add the carrot, parsnip, and celery and cook for 1 minute.

4. Stir in the flour, followed by the beef stock, wine, tomato paste, and Worcestershire sauce, stirring to incorporate the flour and tomato paste fully.

5. Carefully add the stew beef, bay leaf, and potato to the stew. Once it begins to simmer, adjust the heat to low, cover the pot, and cook for 2 hours. Let cool slightly before serving.

> **KITCHEN HACK:** If you have a multi-cooker, this is a great recipe to leave cooking all day on the slow-cook function. You'll want to brown the beef as outlined in steps 1 and 2 to build flavor, then place all the ingredients in the cooker in the order listed. Cover the cooker, set it to Slow Cook, and set the time for 8 hours on low or 5 hours on high.

For the Sous Chef:

Prep the ingredients by cubing the beef, mincing the garlic, and dicing the carrot, parsnip, celery, and potato. .

CARBONARA RISOTTO

SERVES 2 | PREP TIME: 10 MINUTES | COOK TIME: 35 MINUTES

Cozy Comforts, Date Night, Gluten Free, Nut Free

Is there anything more romantic than a rich, creamy risotto? This carbonara version is decadent and delicious without being overly complicated. Cooking risotto may sound like a long, laborious process, but this version requires only a few ingredients and takes just over 30 minutes. Once you have mastered it, try swapping out the pancetta for mushrooms and chicken or shrimp and asparagus.

1 TABLESPOON UNSALTED BUTTER, DIVIDED

1 GARLIC CLOVE, MINCED

1 WHITE ONION, DICED AND DIVIDED

¾ CUP ARBORIO RICE

1 CUP WHITE WINE

SEA SALT

FRESHLY GROUND BLACK PEPPER

2 CUPS CHICKEN STOCK

1 TEASPOON VINEGAR

2 EGGS

1 TABLESPOON EXTRA-VIRGIN OLIVE OIL

¼ CUP DICED PANCETTA

½ CUP HALF-AND-HALF

½ CUP GRATED PARMESAN CHEESE

1. In a medium nonstick pan over medium heat, melt 1 tablespoon of butter. Add the garlic and sauté for 30 seconds. Add half the diced onion and cook for 1 minute more.

2. Add the rice and toss until it is evenly mixed with the butter, garlic, and onion. Add the wine, season with salt and pepper, and cook, stirring continuously. When most of the liquid has absorbed into the rice, add ½ cup of chicken stock. Repeat with the remaining stock until the rice has cooked through and the mixture begins to get creamy, about 30 minutes total.

3. Bring a large pot of water to a boil over high heat. Add the vinegar and turn down the heat so the water is barely simmering. Gently crack the eggs into the water and let them poach until firm on the outside, no more than 3 minutes. Using a slotted spoon, remove and set aside on a plate.

4. In a separate pan over medium heat, heat the olive oil. Add the remaining onion and the pancetta and cook for 5 to 6 minutes, until the pancetta is browned and starting to crisp. Add the half-and-half and cook for 4 minutes to reduce.

5. Stir the pancetta-cream mixture directly into the risotto, folding it in until the pancetta is evenly distributed.

6. Spoon the risotto into two bowls and top each with a poached egg.

> **MIX IT UP:** If you have limited stovetop space or cookware, skip step 3 and, instead, fry the eggs in the same pan used to cook the pancetta cream at the end of step 4.

For the Sous Chef:

Prep the ingredients by mincing the garlic and dicing and dividing the onion. While the chef is working on the risotto in step 2, complete steps 3 and 4 so when the risotto is done absorbing all the liquid, the meal will come together at the same time.

CREAMY TOMATO & SAUSAGE RIGATONI

SERVES 2 | PREP TIME: 10 MINUTES | COOK TIME: 40 MINUTES

Cozy Comforts, Nut Free, Weeknight

When you find a signature dish at your favorite restaurant, it can be difficult to deviate. Such is the case with Julien and "The Rigatoni." Despite an ever-changing seasonal menu at this favorite French bistro of ours, the rigatoni in a creamy tomato and sausage sauce will always be part of our order. While we have never actually asked for the recipe, Julien has had it enough times to make it on his own.

1 TABLESPOON EXTRA-VIRGIN OLIVE OIL

8 OUNCES GROUND SWEET ITALIAN SAUSAGE

½ YELLOW ONION, CHOPPED

1 GARLIC CLOVE, MINCED

1½ CUPS MARINARA SAUCE

8 OUNCES DRY RIGATONI PASTA

1 CUP RICOTTA

½ CUP GRATED PARMESAN CHEESE

2 TABLESPOONS CHOPPED FRESH PARSLEY

¼ CUP SHREDDED MOZZARELLA CHEESE

3 SLICES PROVOLONE CHEESE

1. Preheat the oven to 375°F.

2. In a large skillet over medium-high heat, heat the olive oil. Add the sausage to the skillet and cook for 5 minutes or until browned.

3. Add the onion and garlic to the sausage and cook for 5 to 6 minutes, until the onion is translucent. Stir in the marinara sauce and cook until the sauce is warm. Remove the skillet from the heat.

4. Bring a large pot of water to a boil over high heat. Cook the rigatoni for 5 minutes (it will be very al dente). Drain and return to the pot.

5. In a small bowl, stir together the ricotta, Parmesan cheese, and parsley until fully combined.

6. Add the sausage sauce and the ricotta mixture to the pot with the rigatoni and mix well to coat the pasta fully.

7. Pour the pasta mixture into a small baking dish. Sprinkle the mozzarella cheese all over the top and layer the provolone slices on top of the mozzarella.

8. Bake, uncovered, for 20 minutes, until the cheese is golden and bubbling. Let cool for at least 5 minutes before serving.

SWAP IT OUT: If you love spicy food, try swapping the sweet Italian sausage for the hot variety. You can also sub ground beef for the sausage.

For the Sous Chef:

Prep the ingredients by mincing the garlic, chopping the onion, chopping the parsley, and decasing the sausage (if you are unable to find ground sausage). Then, jump ahead to steps 4 and 5 to get the pasta water boiling and the cheese ready while the chef cooks the sausage.

GARLIC & HERB FILET MIGNON

SERVES 2 | PREP TIME: 5 MINUTES | COOK TIME: 10 MINUTES

Cozy Comforts, Date Night, Gluten Free, Nut Free, Weeknight

Filet mignon may sound fancy, but this tender cut of beef is relatively easy to make—even by the most novice cook. We can't think of a more romantic meal for two to enjoy on special occasions, such as date night, Valentine's Day, or birthdays. Serve with Parmesan Roasted Asparagus (page 50) and Grilled Chicken & Romaine Caesar (page 42, just omit the chicken). Be sure to open a bottle of dry red wine to serve alongside.

1 GARLIC CLOVE, MINCED

1 TEASPOON FINELY CHOPPED FRESH BASIL

1 TEASPOON FINELY CHOPPED FRESH THYME LEAVES

1 TEASPOON FINELY CHOPPED FRESH ROSEMARY

2 (4-OUNCE) BEEF FILETS

SEA SALT

FRESHLY GROUND BLACK PEPPER

1 TABLESPOON UNSALTED BUTTER

1. In a small bowl, stir together the garlic, basil, thyme, and rosemary.

2. Season the steaks with salt and pepper, then rub the garlic and herb mix evenly onto all sides of the filets.

3. In a large nonstick skillet over medium-high heat, melt the butter. Once the skillet is hot and the butter is melted, add the filets and cook for 4 minutes per side for a medium-rare steak. Adjust the cook time depending on your desired doneness.

For the Sous Chef:

Prep the ingredients by mincing the garlic and chopping the basil, thyme, and rosemary.

FALAFEL GYROS WITH TZATZIKI

SERVES 2 | PREP TIME: 15 MINUTES, PLUS OVERNIGHT TO SOAK |
COOK TIME: 10 MINUTES

Meatless Monday, Nut Free, Weeknight

Made from chickpeas, falafel is brown and crisp on the outside and warm and soft on the inside. It can be served as a platter over a bed of rice, but we find it is best enjoyed in a gyro—a Mediterranean sandwich. In this version, warm pita bread is stuffed with crispy hot falafel balls, cool diced tomato, diced cucumber, and sliced onion and topped with creamy tzatziki sauce to pull it all together. Enjoy at home for dinner or pack the gyros for an easy lunch on the go.

FOR THE FALAFEL

1/3 CUP DRIED CHICKPEAS, SOAKED IN 1½ CUPS WATER OVERNIGHT AND DRAINED

1 EGG

2 GARLIC CLOVES, PEELED

½ SHALLOT, CHOPPED

1 TABLESPOON FRESH PARSLEY

1 TABLESPOON ALL-PURPOSE FLOUR

½ TEASPOON GROUND CUMIN

½ TEASPOON GROUND CORIANDER

SEA SALT

FRESHLY GROUND BLACK PEPPER

VEGETABLE OIL, FOR FRYING

FOR THE GYROS

2 PITA BREAD ROUNDS

½ CUP TZATZIKI (PAGE 184)

1 TOMATO, DICED

½ RED ONION, SLICED

½ CUCUMBER, DICED

¼ CUP CRUMBLED FETA CHEESE

TO MAKE THE FALAFEL

1. In a food processor, combine the drained chickpeas, egg, garlic, shallot, parsley, flour, cumin, and coriander, and season with salt and pepper. Blend the ingredients until well combined, creating a thick paste.

2. In a cast-iron skillet over medium-high heat, heat 1 inch of vegetable oil.

3. Using your hands, form the falafel mixture into balls about 1½ inches in diameter.

(Continued)

4. Carefully place the falafel balls into the hot oil and fry for about 5 minutes or until golden brown, turning while you cook. Using a slotted spoon, transfer them to a paper towel–lined plate to drain.

To assemble the gyros

1. Place two pieces of aluminum foil on a flat surface. Lay one pita bread round in the center of each. Spread ¼ cup of tzatziki onto each pita and top each with half the tomato, red onion, cucumber, and feta cheese.

2. Add 3 or 4 falafel balls to each pita. Roll each sandwich up and wrap it with the foil, ensuring that one end of the pita is fully enclosed by the foil so none of the toppings fall out.

For the Sous Chef:

Prep the ingredients by dicing the tomato and slicing the red onion for the toppings. Prepare the pita bread in step 1 (assemble gyros) while the chef is working on forming and frying the falafel.

SUMMER VEGGIE ORECCHIETTE & PESTO

SERVES 2 | PREP TIME: 10 MINUTES | COOK TIME: 15 MINUTES

Meatless Monday, Weeknight

Pasta is traditionally viewed as a rich comfort food, meaning that it can be overlooked on summer nights when all you want is a simple dish that takes little effort. But, if we're being honest, we would eat pasta every night! And this orecchiette dish can be a summer weeknight savior. Packed full of fresh vegetables, basil pesto, and just a pinch of Parmesan cheese, this dish can also be customized to include just about any vegetable you happen to be craving or growing in abundance.

1 EAR OF CORN, HUSKED, ALL SILKS REMOVED

6 OUNCES DRY ORECCHIETTE PASTA

2 TABLESPOONS EXTRA-VIRGIN OLIVE OIL

½ CUP FRESH PEAS

1 CUP CHERRY TOMATOES, QUARTERED

2 TABLESPOONS GRATED PARMESAN CHEESE

⅓ CUP 5-INGREDIENT PESTO (SEE PAGE 185)

SEA SALT

FRESHLY GROUND BLACK PEPPER

1. Cut the corn kernels off the cob and set aside. Discard the cob.

2. Bring a large pot of water to a boil over high heat. Cook the orecchiette pasta according to the package directions, reducing the cooking time by 1 minute so the pasta is just al dente. Reserve ¼ cup of the pasta water. Drain and return the pasta to the pot.

3. In a medium pan over medium-high heat, heat the olive oil. Add the corn in an even layer and cook for 1 minute without stirring.

4. Add the peas, stir to combine, and cook for 1 minute.

5. Turn the heat under the pasta to medium. Stir in the corn and peas, tomatoes, 2 tablespoons of reserved pasta water, the Parmesan cheese, and pesto, stirring constantly to ensure all the pasta is coated. Cook for 2 minutes or until the tomatoes begin to soften.

(Continued)

6. If the pasta seems dry, gradually add the remaining 2 tablespoons of pasta water until you have the consistency you like. Season with salt and pepper to taste.

> **INGREDIENT TIP:** It isn't always easy to find fresh corn on the cob or peas throughout the year. If you're craving the summertime flavors of this dish but can't find fresh corn or peas, we recommend skipping the canned versions and using frozen varieties instead. Make sure you factor in time for them to defrost before you start cooking.

For the Sous Chef:

Prep the ingredients by quartering the cherry tomatoes. Then, jump right into husking and cutting the corn in step 1 and boiling the water in step 2 so the chef can start on step 3.

CAULIFLOWER & RICOTTA PIZZA

SERVES 2 | PREP TIME: 10 MINUTES | COOK TIME: 45 MINUTES

Cozy Comforts, Meatless Monday, Nut Free

Making pizza at home is the quintessential date night in, but that doesn't mean you have to make the dough from scratch and have a flour fight, like in the movies. Instead, we opt for a premade dough (from the grocery store or your local pizza joint) and spend time on the toppings. In this pizza, we amp up the cauliflower in a bright, salty marinade that pairs perfectly with creamy ricotta. All you need to round out this meal is a bottle of your favorite vino and Coffee Crème Brûlée (page 108) for dessert.

ALL-PURPOSE FLOUR, FOR DUSTING

½ STORE-BOUGHT PIZZA DOUGH BALL

JUICE OF ½ LEMON

2 GARLIC CLOVES, PEELED

3 TABLESPOONS CAPERS, DRAINED

2 TABLESPOONS EXTRA-VIRGIN OLIVE OIL

SEA SALT

FRESHLY GROUND BLACK PEPPER

½ HEAD CAULIFLOWER, CUT INTO FLORETS

¾ CUP SHREDDED MOZZARELLA CHEESE

½ CUP RICOTTA

½ CUP UNSEASONED BREAD CRUMBS

¼ CUP GRATED PARMESAN CHEESE

1. Preheat the oven to 400°F.

2. Dust a work surface with flour and place the pizza dough on it. Roll the dough into a 10-inch circle, ensuring the thickness of the dough is consistent. Transfer to a baking sheet and set aside.

3. In a blender or food processor, combine the lemon juice, garlic, capers, and olive oil; season with salt and pepper. Blend until the ingredients form a loose paste.

4. Transfer the paste to a large bowl and add the cauliflower. Toss together, making sure all the florets are coated. Transfer to another baking sheet and roast for 20 minutes or until the cauliflower is tender.

5. Turn the oven up to 525°F or as high as your oven temperature will go. Place the rack in the lower half of the oven.

6. Cover the pizza dough with the mozzarella cheese. Using a spoon, dot the top of the dough with the ricotta. Top that with the cauliflower mixture. Bake for 15 to 20 minutes, until the crust is golden brown.

(Continued)

CAULIFLOWER & RICOTTA PIZZA *(Continued)*

7. Remove the pizza from the oven and carefully sprinkle the bread crumbs and Parmesan cheese on top. Return to the oven and bake for 3 minutes more.

For the Sous Chef:

Prep the ingredients by chopping the cauliflower into florets. Then, jump to step 3 and make the paste while the chef is rolling out the pizza dough. Work together in step 6 to add the toppings to the crust.

CACIO E PEPE

SERVES 2 | PREP TIME: 10 MINUTES | COOK TIME: 20 MINUTES

Cozy Comforts, Meatless Monday, Nut Free, Weeknight

Christmas came pretty quickly after our wedding, and because we had received some great kitchenware from our registry, we didn't really have an answer when family members asked us what we wanted for holiday gifts. So when Kenzie told her grandmother she wanted a giant wheel of Parmigiano-Reggiano, we didn't think she would actually *take her up on the suggestion. We've been trying to come up with many creative ways to use as much of the wheel as possible over the past few months, and this simple Italian pasta has been an oft-repeated meal to help with our cheesy mission. Buon appetito!*

SEA SALT

6 OUNCES DRY LONG PASTA (SUCH AS SPAGHETTI, THICK SPAGHETTI, LINGUINI, OR BUCATINI)

3 TABLESPOONS UNSALTED BUTTER, DIVIDED

1 TEASPOON FRESHLY GROUND BLACK PEPPER

¾ CUP FINELY GRATED PARMIGIANO-REGGIANO CHEESE

¼ CUP FINELY GRATED PECORINO ROMANO CHEESE

1. In a large pot over high heat, bring 3 quarts water to a rolling boil. Season with salt and add the pasta. Cook for 2 minutes less than the package directions suggest, stirring occasionally to prevent the noodles from sticking. Reserve ¾ cup of the cooking water, drain the pasta, and set aside.

2. In a large skillet over medium heat, melt 2 tablespoons of butter. Add the pepper and, cook for 1 minute, stirring continuously.

3. Add half the reserved pasta water to the skillet and bring to a simmer. Place the drained pasta and remaining 1 tablespoon of butter in the skillet and toss to combine.

4. Reduce the heat to low and slowly add the Parmigiano-Reggiano cheese while tossing the pasta with tongs. Toss, mixing, until the cheese is fully melted.

(Continued)

5. Remove the pan from the heat and slowly add the Pecorino Romano cheese, continuing to toss to melt the cheese. Add the remaining pasta water if the cheese is not melting as quickly.

> **INGREDIENT TIP:** If you have a great supermarket or cheese shop nearby with many selections, you can swap out the Parmigiano-Reggiano for Grana Padano—another hard Italian cheese that has a slightly milder flavor.

For the Sous Chef:

The perfect cacio e pepe comes to life through slowly adding the cheese so it can melt and create a sauce. While the chef tosses the pasta, the sous chef can help by gradually adding the cheese in steps 4 and 5.

LOAF PAN EGGPLANT LASAGNA

SERVES 2 | PREP TIME: 35 MINUTES | COOK TIME: 40 MINUTES

Cozy Comforts, Date Night, Gluten Free, Meatless Monday, Nut Free

This vegetarian dish has all the cheesy, saucy goodness you'd expect from lasagna, but without the heaviness of pasta noodles. Instead, thinly sliced eggplant takes center stage in its place. Not only is this a twist on a traditional lasagna because of the ingredients, but it is made in a loaf pan—the perfect size for two portions. When you and your significant other are craving a comforting meal, this one is sure to satisfy.

1 MEDIUM (6- TO 8-INCH-LONG) EGGPLANT, TRIMMED AND PEELED

SEA SALT

1 TABLESPOON EXTRA-VIRGIN OLIVE OIL

2 GARLIC CLOVES, MINCED

½ YELLOW ONION, CHOPPED

1 TEASPOON DRIED BASIL

FRESHLY GROUND BLACK PEPPER

1½ CUPS MARINARA SAUCE

1 CUP RICOTTA

¼ CUP GRATED PARMESAN CHEESE

1 EGG

2 TABLESPOONS CHOPPED FRESH PARSLEY

2 CUPS SHREDDED MOZZARELLA CHEESE

1. Preheat the oven to 400°F.

2. Cut the eggplant into thin "sheets" from end to end (⅛ to ¼ inch thick), to create long slices that resemble lasagna noodles.

3. Lay the eggplant slices on a baking sheet and sprinkle the tops with salt. Let sit for 15 minutes, flip, and sprinkle the other side with salt. Let sit for 15 minutes more. Using a paper towel, pat each piece dry and brush off any residual salt.

4. In a large pan over medium heat, heat the olive oil. Add the garlic and sauté for 1 minute. Add the onion and basil and season with pepper. Cook for 3 to 4 minutes, until the onion is translucent.

5. Stir in the marinara sauce and continue to cook until the sauce is warm.

6. In a medium bowl, combine the ricotta, Parmesan cheese, egg, and parsley; stir until fully combined.

(Continued)

7. In a 9-by-5-inch loaf plan, spread a spoonful of the marinara sauce to cover the bottom. Layer one eggplant slice on top, then spread a layer of the ricotta mixture. Sprinkle some mozzarella cheese on top. Repeat the layers—marinara sauce, eggplant, ricotta, mozzarella cheese—until you have reached the top of the pan or used up your ingredients.

8. Cover the pan with aluminum foil and bake for 25 to 30 minutes.

> **PREP TIP:** We find that salting the eggplant and letting it rest, or "sweating" it, helps bring out the flavor of the eggplant and keep this lasagna more formed once you cut into it. If you're in a time crunch but still want to enjoy this recipe, skip the sweating but expect a "looser" final product.

For the Sous Chef:

Prep the ingredients by mincing the garlic and chopping the onion and parsley. While the chef is working on building the sauce in steps 4 and 5, make the ricotta mixture in step 6.

HONEY SRIRACHA-GLAZED SALMON

SERVES 2 | 5 MINUTES PLUS 1 HOUR TO MARINATE | COOK TIME: 12 TO 14 MINUTES

Dairy Free, Date Night, Nut Free

We love salmon for its versatility: You can pan-fry it to get a nice crisp, grill it in the summertime, or even steam it. This version packs a punch by combining fiery Sriracha with salty soy sauce and super sweet honey—it's the best of all taste worlds combined! And because you bake it right on parchment paper, cleaning up couldn't be easier.

2 (4-OUNCE) SALMON FILLETS

2 TABLESPOONS SOY SAUCE

1 TABLESPOON HONEY

1½ TEASPOONS RICE VINEGAR

1½ TEASPOONS SRIRACHA

1 GARLIC CLOVE, MINCED

1. Place the salmon fillets in a rimmed baking dish.

2. In a medium bowl, whisk the soy sauce, honey, vinegar, Sriracha, and garlic. Pour the mixture over the salmon so the fillets are evenly coated. Refrigerate for 1 hour, turning the salmon once.

3. Preheat the oven to 425°F. Line a baking sheet with parchment paper.

4. Transfer the salmon to the prepared baking sheet and bake for 12 to 14 minutes, until the salmon is flaky.

> **PREP TIP:** If you know you're not going to have a ton of time to marinate when you get home from work, build the marinade in the morning and let the fish rest in it for up to 8 hours before cooking.

For the Sous Chef:

While the chef is taking care of the salmon, assemble a simple salad or cook brown rice to accompany the meal.

MUSSELS IN WHITE WINE & GARLIC WITH CRUSTY BREAD

SERVES 2 | PREP TIME: 10 MINUTES | COOK TIME: 15 MINUTES

Cozy Comforts, Date Night, Meatless Monday, One Pot, Weeknight

This recipe is a twist on a traditional French dish, mussels mariniere, *or* moules marinières. *This version is an easy one-pot meal that's ready in just 15 minutes and requires just a few simple ingredients. It makes for the perfect light appetizer, or it can be combined with pasta for a hearty entrée. All you need is a big pot and you're ready to go! Don't forget the crusty bread, perfect for soaking up every last bit of the savory white wine and garlic sauce.*

2 POUNDS LIVE MUSSELS

1 CUP DRY WHITE WINE

3 GARLIC CLOVES, MINCED

1 TABLESPOON MINCED WHITE ONION

SEA SALT

FRESHLY GROUND BLACK PEPPER

3 TABLESPOONS UNSALTED BUTTER

2 TABLESPOONS CHOPPED FRESH PARSLEY

1 TEASPOON DRIED BASIL

½ BAGUETTE, FRENCH BREAD LOAF, OR OTHER CRUSTY BREAD LOAF, SLICED

1. Place the mussels in a colander and rinse them under cold water, gently shaking to ensure all are clean. Using a small, sharp knife, carefully scrape any dirt and beards (strings) off the shells.

2. Using your fingernail, tap any mussel that is already open. If it doesn't close when you tap it, discard it.

3. In a large pot over medium heat, combine the wine, garlic, and onion and season with salt and pepper. Bring to a simmer and cook for 5 minutes.

4. Carefully add the mussels to the pot, cover, and turn the heat to high. Cook for 5 minutes.

5. Stir in the butter, parsley, and basil and remove the pan from the heat. Remove and discard any mussels that haven't opened during the cooking process.

6. Divide the mussels and broth evenly between two bowls and serve with the sliced bread.

FOR A CROWD: This is one of those meals that strikes a great balance between seeming like something you'd find at a fancy restaurant and being easy and quick to make. You can easily double or triple this recipe to impress friends and family who come over for dinner any night of the week—just make sure you have a big enough pot.

For the Sous Chef:

Clean the mussels in steps 1 and 2 while the chef preps for step 3 by mincing the garlic and onion. While the chef is working on the wine broth in step 3, chop the parsley.

COD & VEGETABLES EN PAPILLOTE

SERVES 2 | PREP TIME: 5 MINUTES | COOK TIME: 12 MINUTES

Dairy Free, Gluten Free, Meatless Monday, Nut Free, One Pot, Weeknight

En papillote may sound like a fancy French cooking technique, but the truth is that cooking "in parchment" yields big reward without much effort—and cleanup is a breeze! The folded parchment does all the work locking in flavor and moisture. When cooking for two, you can either make two separate packets or one big one.

8 ASPARAGUS SPEARS, ROUGH ENDS TRIMMED

2 CARROTS, CUT INTO MATCHSTICKS

2 (6-OUNCE) COD FILLETS

2 ROUND LEMON SLICES

SEA SALT

FRESHLY GROUND BLACK PEPPER

2 TABLESPOONS FRESHLY SQUEEZED LEMON JUICE

2 TABLESPOONS EXTRA-VIRGIN OLIVE OIL

2 ROSEMARY SPRIGS

1. Preheat the oven to 350°F. Place a large sheet pan in the oven to preheat.

2. Fold two 14-by-12-inch pieces of parchment paper in half. Using kitchen shears, cut each piece of parchment into a heart shape and unfold.

3. For each packet: Arrange the asparagus and carrots tightly together on one side of the paper heart. Season with salt. Place the cod fillet on top of the veggies, add a lemon slice, and season with salt, pepper, and a tablespoon each of lemon juice and olive oil. Top with a rosemary sprig.

4. Fold one side of the heart shape over the fish and, working from one end, tightly fold the open edge of the paper to form a seal.

5. Transfer the packets to the preheated sheet pan. Bake for 12 minutes. Remove pan and let cool for 3 minutes.

6. Carefully open the paper packets, keeping your hands and face away from the steam.

For the Sous Chef:

Prep the ingredients by trimming the asparagus, peeling, trimming, and cutting the carrots, and slicing the lemon. You can each create your own packet in steps 3 through 5.

SHRIMP PAD THAI

SERVES 2 | PREP TIME: 10 MINUTES | COOK TIME: 15 MINUTES

Cozy Comforts, Dairy Free, Gluten Free, Weeknight

This is what we like to call a "takeout fakeout." This pad thai recipe takes less time than delivery, and it is so much cheaper to make at home (using better quality ingredients!). Sticky, sweet, and perfectly salty, this is our go-to when we crave some fast indulgence but don't want the guilt. Bring a little flair to the table by serving this dish in takeout boxes with chopsticks.

4 OUNCES RICE NOODLES, LABELED AS STIR-FRY OR PAD THAI NOODLES

2 TABLESPOONS FRESHLY SQUEEZED LIME JUICE

1½ TABLESPOONS PACKED LIGHT BROWN SUGAR

1 TABLESPOON FISH SAUCE

1 TEASPOON RED PEPPER FLAKES

2 TABLESPOONS VEGETABLE OIL, PLUS 1 TEASPOON

1 SHALLOT, THINLY SLICED

2 GARLIC CLOVES, MINCED

8 OUNCES MEDIUM UNCOOKED SHRIMP, SHELLED AND DEVEINED

1 EGG, BEATEN

2 SCALLIONS, THINLY SLICED

PEANUTS, FOR GARNISH

BEAN SPROUTS, FOR GARNISH

CHOPPED FRESH CILANTRO, FOR GARNISH

LIME WEDGES, FOR GARNISH

1. Place the rice noodles in a large bowl and add enough hot water to cover. Let soak for 5 minutes, drain, and set aside.

2. In a small bowl, whisk together the lime juice, brown sugar, fish sauce, and red pepper flakes until well combined.

3. In a large skillet over high heat, heat 2 tablespoons of vegetable oil. Add the shallot and garlic and cook for 3 minutes or until slightly browned.

4. Add the rice noodles. Cook, stirring frequently, for 2 minutes.

5. Add the shrimp. Cook, stirring occasionally, until they begin to curl, about 2 minutes.

6. Push the noodles and shrimp to one side of the skillet and add the remaining 1 teaspoon of vegetable oil to the other side. Carefully add the egg and scramble for 1 minute or until it is almost firm. Add the scallions to the skillet and toss together all the ingredients.

7. Pour the lime juice mixture into the skillet and cook, stirring frequently, for 2 minutes or until the ingredients are evenly coated with the sauce.

8. Transfer the pad thai to two bowls and garnish with peanuts, bean sprouts, cilantro, and lime wedges for squeezing.

For the Sous Chef:

Prep the ingredients by slicing the shallot and scallions, mincing the garlic, and beating the egg. Then move on to step 1 so your chef can begin building the sauce in step 2. While your chef is stir-frying the pad thai, chop the cilantro and cut the lime wedges.

BAKED LOBSTER MACARONI & CHEESE

SERVES 2 | PREP TIME: 10 MINUTES | COOK TIME: 35 MINUTES

Cozy Comforts, Date Night, Nut Free

Luscious and creamy, this outrageously cheesy sauce pairs perfectly with rich, buttery lobster, proving that seafood and cheese can come together harmoniously. While the richness of the lobster marries well with the cheddar and Gruyère, it is the crunchy bread crumb topping that sets this apart. It's a perfect choice when you want to wow your significant other with a decadent date night in.

8 OUNCES DRY ELBOW MACARONI

1 TABLESPOON UNSALTED BUTTER

1 TABLESPOON ALL-PURPOSE FLOUR

¾ CUP WHOLE MILK

SEA SALT

FRESHLY GROUND BLACK PEPPER

¼ CUP SHREDDED CHEDDAR CHEESE

¼ CUP SHREDDED GRUYÈRE CHEESE

¼ CUP GRATED PARMESAN CHEESE

4 OUNCES COOKED LOBSTER, CHOPPED

2 TABLESPOONS UNSEASONED BREAD CRUMBS

½ TEASPOON EXTRA-VIRGIN OLIVE OIL

1. Preheat the oven to 375°F.

2. Bring a large pot of salted water to a boil over high heat. Cook the elbow macaroni according to the package directions, subtracting 1 minute from the cooking time. Drain and set aside.

3. In a large saucepan over medium heat, melt the butter. To create a roux, sprinkle the flour over the butter and cook for about 2 minutes, stirring constantly, until the mixture is golden in color.

4. Add the milk to the roux and whisk until combined. Season with salt and pepper. Simmer for about 2 minutes to allow the roux to thicken.

5. Remove the pan from the heat and whisk in the cheddar, Gruyère, and Parmesan cheeses, whisking until completely smooth.

6. Add the cooked pasta and lobster to the pan and stir until well combined. Spoon the pasta mixture into two ramekins, dividing evenly.

7. In a small bowl, stir together the bread crumbs and olive oil; season with salt and pepper. Sprinkle the mixture on top of each filled ramekin.

8. Bake the ramekins for 15 minutes or until the cheese is bubbling and the bread crumbs are golden brown.

SWAP IT OUT: Is one of you a seafood lover, while the other could do without it? This mac and cheese recipe makes the perfect base for any protein—or tastes great by itself. Sub in cooked chicken or bacon for a different flavor!

For the Sous Chef:

Preheat the oven and prep the ingredients by grating and shredding the cheeses and chopping the lobster. Help your chef get ready to put the macaroni and cheese in the oven by jumping ahead to step 7 to create the crunchy topping.

Desserts for Two

STRAWBERRY-BASIL SORBET — 105

CHOCOLATE MOUSSE — 106

BREAD PUDDING FOR TWO — 107

COFFEE CRÈME BRÛLÉE — 108

STRAWBERRY SHORTCAKE — 110

PEACH & RASPBERRY COBBLER — 112

MINI CHEESECAKES — 114

MUG BROWNIES À LA MODE — 116

STRACCIATELLA SEMIFREDDO — 118

CHOCOLATE CHIP SKILLET COOKIE — 119

STRAWBERRY-BASIL SORBET

SERVES 2 | PREP TIME: 10 MINUTES

Dairy Free, Date Night, Gluten Free, Nut Free, One Pot

Gone are the days when you needed to register for kitchen appliances that serve one purpose only. No one really needs an ice cream maker or bread machine collecting dust and taking up space in the pantry, only to be used once or twice a year. Instead, unlock the versatility of your new high-speed blender or food processor and make a delicious and refreshing frozen treat.

1½ CUPS FROZEN STRAWBERRIES

½ CUP COCONUT WATER

1 TABLESPOON FRESHLY SQUEEZED LEMON JUICE

1 TEASPOON LEMON ZEST

3 OR 4 FRESH BASIL LEAVES, CHOPPED

1. In a high-speed blender or food processor, combine the strawberries, coconut water, lemon juice, lemon zest, and basil. Blend until thick and smooth, scraping down the sides of the blender if needed.

2. Divide the sorbet between two bowls. Serve immediately.

> **MIX IT UP:** Use this recipe as a formula to make a variety of frozen treats with whatever frozen fruit you have on hand! Use coconut milk instead of coconut water for a thicker consistency, or mix in chocolate chips in place of the basil. The options are endless.

For the Sous Chef:

Prep the ingredients by juicing and zesting the lemon.

CHOCOLATE MOUSSE

SERVES 2 | PREP TIME: 5 MINUTES | COOK TIME: 5 MINUTES

Date Night, Gluten Free, Nut Free

There is something inherently romantic about chocolate mousse that makes it our go-to dessert, whether it is Valentine's Day or a date-night dinner at home. The rich chocolate combines with thick cream to create a decadent, velvety-smooth dessert sure to satisfy any sweet tooth. Enjoy it topped with fresh cream or fresh berries.

1 CUP MILK CHOCOLATE CHIPS

1 TABLESPOON UNSALTED BUTTER

1 EGG YOLK

½ CUP HEAVY (WHIPPING) CREAM, CHILLED

1 TABLESPOON POWDERED SUGAR

1. In a medium glass bowl, melt the chocolate chips and butter in the microwave on 50 percent power in 30-second increments, stopping to stir after each, until the mixture is smooth. Place a mug of water in the microwave (but not too close to the chocolate) to ensure a moist environment.

2. Stir the egg yolk into the melted chocolate.

3. In another medium bowl, using a handheld electric mixer, whip the chilled heavy cream on high speed until soft peaks form.

4. Add the powdered sugar and melted chocolate to the whipped cream. Beat the chocolate into the cream mixture until fully incorporated. Divide the mousse between two small bowls.

For the Sous Chef:

Prep the ingredients by separating the egg. Proceed to step 3 and whip the heavy cream while the chef completes steps 1 and 2.

BREAD PUDDING FOR TWO

MAKES 4 MINI BREAD PUDDING CUPS, SERVING 2 | PREP TIME: 5 MINUTES |
COOK TIME: 40 MINUTES

Cozy Comforts, Date Night, Meatless Monday, Nut Free

Julien's work brings him to Auburn, Alabama, a few times a year. It's a great change of pace (and weather) from the bustle of Boston—not to mention, delicious food choices abound. One of his coworkers who grew up in London recommended a restaurant, making the bold claim that their bread pudding was the best thing he'd ever eaten in America, so Julien knew he had to try it. Served in a ramekin and topped with a delicious sauce, it lived up to the hype. This recipe was inspired by that delicious dish, and we've built our version in muffin tins so the cleanup is easy and you can even take any leftovers to go!

2 SLICES DAY-OLD BREAD, CUBED

1 CUP MILK

2 EGGS

¼ CUP SUGAR

½ TEASPOON GROUND CINNAMON

⅛ TEASPOON SEA SALT

MAPLE SYRUP, FOR FINISHING

1. Preheat the oven to 350°F. Line four wells of a muffin tin with paper liners.

2. Divide the bread cubes among the four lined wells.

3. In a medium bowl, whisk together the milk, eggs, sugar, cinnamon, and salt until the eggs are fully incorporated. Pour the wet mixture over the bread cubes.

4. Bake for 40 minutes. When done, the tops will be browned and the edges crispy. Drizzle with maple syrup before serving.

For the Sous Chef:

Prep the ingredients by cutting the bread so the chef can whisk the wet ingredients.

COFFEE CRÈME BRÛLÉE

SERVES 2 | PREP TIME: 10 MINUTES | COOK TIME: 45 MINUTES

Cozy Comforts, Date Night, Gluten Free, Meatless Monday, Nut Free

A rich custard base topped with caramelized sugar, this dessert is a classic for a reason. Often enjoyed as a special treat when we go out to eat, it took years before we tried to make it at home. In fact, there is a little spot in our old neighborhood that inspired this twist on the classic. Whenever we are there, we always order the Coffee Crème Brûlée and two spoons, no matter how full we are. Using the oven's broiler, you can easily replicate the classic technique and make this restaurant-style dessert at home.

2 EGG YOLKS

8 TABLESPOONS SUGAR, DIVIDED

¾ CUP HEAVY (WHIPPING) CREAM

1½ TEASPOONS INSTANT COFFEE

¼ TEASPOON VANILLA EXTRACT

1. Preheat the oven to 300°F.

2. In a medium bowl, whisk the egg yolks and 3 tablespoons sugar for 1 minute. Set aside.

3. In a separate bowl, whisk half of the heavy cream with the coffee until the mixture is smooth and the coffee has dissolved. Add the remaining heavy cream and whisk until fully combined.

4. Carefully pour the coffee mixture into the egg yolk mixture and gently fold together.

5. Divide the crème brûlée mixture between two ramekins, being sure not to fill them all the way to the top.

6. Place the ramekins into an oven-safe dish that is slightly larger and has taller sides than the ramekins. Move the dish into the oven. Carefully pour water into the dish to surround the ramekins until the water reaches halfway up the sides.

7. Bake for 40 minutes. Turn the oven to broil and move a rack to the top shelf. Sprinkle the remaining 5 tablespoons of sugar evenly on top of the ramekins. Return the dish to the oven and place it on the top shelf, about 1 inch below the broiler. Broil until the tops of the crèmes brûlées begin to brown and the sugar is caramelized.

KITCHEN HACK: If you have a mini kitchen torch, skip the broiling in step 7 and use it to carefully caramelize the sugar atop each ramekin.

For the Sous Chef:

Prep the ingredients by measuring and dividing the sugar. While the chef is whisking the eggs and sugar in step 2, jump ahead to step 3 to work on the coffee mixture.

STRAWBERRY SHORTCAKE

SERVES 2 | PREP TIME: 10 MINUTES | COOK TIME: 8 TO 10 MINUTES

Cozy Comforts, Meatless Monday, Nut Free, Weeknight

Strawberry shortcake screams summer—from the taste of fresh berries to the cool whipped cream. It's perfectly suited to finish off a meal on a warm night. The best part? You can whip together those shortcakes in just a few minutes using pantry staples and serve a simple yet elegant and delicious dessert that can easily be for two on a weeknight or 10 for a party! Strawberries are the classic choice for this, but you can get creative with any juicy fruit that's in season, such as peaches, blueberries, or cherries.

¾ CUP FRESH STRAWBERRIES, HULLED AND HALVED

3 TABLESPOONS SUGAR, DIVIDED

1 CUP ALL-PURPOSE FLOUR

1 TEASPOON BAKING POWDER

½ TEASPOON SALT

2 TABLESPOONS UNSALTED BUTTER, CUT INTO 4 PIECES

¼ CUP PLUS 2 TEASPOONS MILK

WHIPPED CREAM, FOR TOPPING

1. Preheat the oven to 450°F. Line a baking sheet with parchment paper and set aside.

2. In a medium bowl, stir together the strawberries and 1 tablespoon of sugar and set aside.

3. In a food processor, combine the flour, baking powder, salt, and remaining 2 tablespoons of sugar. Pulse 1 to 2 times to combine the ingredients. Add the butter pieces and continue pulsing until they are broken up within the dry ingredients.

4. Pour the milk into the food processor and pulse until a dough forms. Carefully remove the dough, divide it in half, and form each piece into a disc. Place them on the prepared baking sheet and bake for 8 to 10 minutes. The tops of the shortcakes will be slightly browned.

5. Let the shortcakes cool. Top with the strawberries and whipped cream.

> **KITCHEN HACK:** If your kitchen space is limited and you do not have a food processor, use a whisk to stir the dry ingredients together in step 3, then use your hands to break the butter apart and stir it in. Whisk the milk into the ingredients in step 4.

For the Sous Chef:

Prep the ingredients by hulling and halving the strawberries, measuring the dry ingredients, cutting the butter, and measuring the milk. The chef can jump ahead to step 3 while you prepare the strawberries in step 2.

PEACH & RASPBERRY COBBLER

SERVES 2 | PREP TIME: 15 MINUTES | COOK TIME: 20 TO 25 MINUTES

Cozy Comforts, Date Night, Nut Free

Peaches are at their peak in warm summer months—ripe and juicy. In this cobbler, the soft, sweet peaches melt into the buttery crisp topping for a dessert so delectable you won't be able to put your spoon down. So how do you make something this perfect even better? Add fresh raspberries for a twist. This twist was inspired by Julien's love for Peach Melba. Don't forget to top it off with a dollop of fresh whipped cream or a scoop of vanilla ice cream!

FOR THE FILLING

1½ CUPS FRESH
PEACHES, SLICED

½ CUP FRESH RASPBERRIES

1 TABLESPOON SUGAR

1 TABLESPOON
ALL-PURPOSE FLOUR

¼ TEASPOON GROUND
CINNAMON

JUICE OF 1 LEMON

FOR THE COBBLER BATTER

1 CUP PLUS 2 TABLESPOONS
ALL-PURPOSE FLOUR

2 TABLESPOONS FINELY
GROUND CORNMEAL

1 TABLESPOON PLUS
1 TEASPOON SUGAR, DIVIDED

½ TEASPOON
BAKING POWDER

¼ TEASPOON BAKING SODA

SEA SALT

2 TABLESPOONS UNSALTED
BUTTER, CUBED

¼ CUP HEAVY
(WHIPPING) CREAM

TO MAKE THE FILLING

1. Preheat the oven to 375°F.

2. In a medium bowl, stir together the peaches, raspberries, sugar, flour, cinnamon, and lemon juice. Divide the filling between two ramekins.

TO MAKE THE COBBLER BATTER

1. In a medium bowl, stir together the flour, cornmeal, 1 tablespoon of sugar, the baking powder, baking soda, and a pinch of salt.

2. Using a pastry cutter or two knives, cut the butter into the flour mixture until it forms an even crumb texture. Stir in the heavy cream until a dough forms.

3. Dollop the dough batter on top of the peach mixture and sprinkle with the remaining 1 teaspoon of sugar.

4. Place the ramekins on a baking sheet and bake for 20 to 25 minutes, until golden brown.

> **SWAP IT OUT:** When peaches and raspberries are no longer in season, transport yourself back to summer using frozen in place of fresh. You can also swap strawberries or blueberries for the peaches.

For the Sous Chef:

Preheat the oven and prep the ingredients by slicing the peaches and measuring the dry ingredients.

MINI CHEESECAKES

MAKES 4 MINI CHEESECAKES, SERVING 2 | PREP TIME: 10 MINUTES |
COOK TIME: 25 MINUTES

Cozy Comforts, Date Night, Meatless Monday, Nut Free

Cheesecake has always been a favorite in our house, but one often reserved for special occasions. The truth is, though, that the buttery crumb crust and rich, creamy center only require a few staple ingredients. We designed this recipe so you can enjoy cheesecake for two, any night of the week. The key to keeping this recipe hassle free? Room temperature ingredients! Take the cream cheese, sour cream, and eggs out of the refrigerator ahead of time to ensure a smooth, velvety texture.

4 GRAHAM CRACKERS, CRUSHED INTO CRUMBS

1½ TABLESPOONS UNSALTED BUTTER, MELTED

6 TEASPOONS SUGAR, DIVIDED

¾ (8-OUNCE) PACKAGE CREAM CHEESE, AT ROOM TEMPERATURE

3 TABLESPOONS SOUR CREAM

1 EGG

¼ TEASPOON VANILLA EXTRACT

FRESH BERRIES, FOR TOPPING

1. Preheat the oven to 325°F. Line four wells of a muffin tin with paper liners and set aside.

2. In a small bowl, stir together the cracker crumbs, melted butter, and 2 teaspoons of sugar until they form a wet, granular mixture. Divide the mixture among the lined muffin wells, pushing it down into the bottom of each cup.

3. Bake for 5 minutes or until the crusts start to brown. Remove and set aside to cool.

4. In the bowl of a stand mixer fitted with the paddle attachment, combine the cream cheese, sour cream, egg, vanilla, and remaining 4 teaspoons of sugar. Beat the ingredients on medium speed until fully combined, scraping down the sides of the bowl as needed to incorporate fully.

5. Pour the cheesecake mixture on top of the cooled crusts, filling each liner almost all the way to the top.

6. Bake for 20 minutes or until the cheesecakes only jiggle slightly when shaking the tin. Remove them from the oven and let them cool completely before serving, topped with the berries.

> **KITCHEN HACK:** Getting a smooth consistency for the filling is the key for a perfect mini cheesecake! If you do not have a stand mixer, use a handheld electric mixer or a sturdy handheld whisk to combine all of the wet ingredients.

For the Sous Chef:

Start on step 2 to create the crusts while the chef starts the cheesecake filling in step 4.

MUG BROWNIES À LA MODE

SERVES 2 | PREP TIME: 5 MINUTES | COOK TIME: 5 MINUTES

Cozy Comforts, Meatless Monday, Nut Free, One Pot, Weeknight

Let's take a moment to honor the genius that came up with the idea to cook dessert in a mug in the microwave. While we can't take credit for the idea, we certainly can get on board. Simply stir a few ingredients together in a mug, and you can have dessert in seconds. What's more, this dessert is perfectly portioned for two.

6 TABLESPOONS SUGAR, DIVIDED

6 TABLESPOONS ALL-PURPOSE FLOUR, DIVIDED

6 TEASPOONS COCOA POWDER, DIVIDED

⅛ TEASPOON SEA SALT, DIVIDED

¼ CUP SEMISWEET CHOCOLATE CHIPS, DIVIDED

3 TABLESPOONS UNSALTED BUTTER, MELTED AND DIVIDED

⅓ CUP MILK, DIVIDED

½ TEASPOON VANILLA EXTRACT, DIVIDED

VANILLA ICE CREAM, FOR SERVING

1. In each of two mugs, stir together 3 tablespoons of sugar, 3 tablespoons of flour, 3 tablespoons of cocoa powder, and half the salt. Add 2 tablespoons of chocolate chips, and stir until the chips are distributed throughout.

2. To each mug add 1½ tablespoons of melted butter, half the milk, and ¼ teaspoon of vanilla. Using a small spatula, stir just until the ingredients are combined.

3. One mug at a time, microwave on 100 percent power for 1 minute. Check on the brownie, microwave it for 15 seconds, and check on it again. Microwave for 15 more seconds or until a toothpick inserted in the center comes out clean. Top with vanilla ice cream and serve.

For the Sous Chef:

The beauty of this recipe is that each person assembles their own mug brownie!

STRACCIATELLA SEMIFREDDO

SERVES 2 | PREP TIME: 10 MINUTES, PLUS 1 HOUR TO FREEZE

Cozy Comforts, Date Night, Gluten Free, Meatless Monday

If you have never tried a semifreddo, you are in for a treat! Semifreddo means "half-cold," or "half-frozen." This classic Italian dessert is somewhere between the texture of a frozen mousse and gelato. In other words, creamy, decadent, and something you are going to love. In this version, chocolate-hazelnut spread is woven throughout and chocolate chips add texture. You can also add your own twist by swapping in whatever toppings and mix-ins you choose. Try fruit, nuts, or your favorite candies.

¼ CUP PLUS 2 TABLESPOONS HEAVY (WHIPPING) CREAM, DIVIDED

1 TABLESPOON POWDERED SUGAR

1 TEASPOON VANILLA EXTRACT

8 TABLESPOONS CREAM CHEESE, AT ROOM TEMPERATURE

2 TABLESPOONS CHOCOLATE-HAZELNUT SPREAD (PAGE 183)

2 TABLESPOONS SEMISWEET CHOCOLATE CHIPS

1. In a medium bowl, combine ¼ cup of heavy cream, the sugar, and vanilla. Using a handheld electric mixer or a stand mixer, beat on high speed until peaks form. Set aside.

2. In a separate bowl, with clean beaters, mix together the cream cheese and remaining 2 tablespoons of heavy cream for 1 minute. Add the chocolate-hazelnut spread and chocolate chips. Using a spatula, evenly distribute the chips throughout the mixture.

3. Using a spatula, fold the whipped cream mixture into the cream cheese mixture. Pour into two small dishes, cover with aluminum foil or plastic wrap, and freeze for 1 hour before serving.

For the Sous Chef:

If you have an extra mixer, jump ahead to step 2 to make the cream cheese mixture while the chef is working on the whipped cream mixture in step 1.

CHOCOLATE CHIP SKILLET COOKIE

SERVES 2 | PREP TIME: 10 MINUTES | COOK TIME: 25 MINUTES

Cozy Comforts, Date Night, Meatless Monday, Nut Free

There's no better way to cure a late-night chocolate craving than a giant cookie that's perfectly crisp on the outside and ooey-gooey on the inside. No need for fancy here. Serve it straight from the skillet with a scoop of ice cream!

½ CUP PLUS 1 TABLESPOON ALL-PURPOSE FLOUR

¼ TEASPOON BAKING SODA

¼ TEASPOON SALT

4 TABLESPOONS UNSALTED BUTTER, AT ROOM TEMPERATURE, DIVIDED

3 TABLESPOONS GRANULATED SUGAR

3 TABLESPOONS PACKED LIGHT BROWN SUGAR

¼ TEASPOON VANILLA EXTRACT

1 EGG

½ CUP SEMISWEET CHOCOLATE CHIPS

1. Preheat the oven to 350°F.

2. In a small bowl, stir together the flour, baking soda, and salt until well combined.

3. In a separate bowl, stir together 2 tablespoons butter, the granulated sugar, brown sugar, and vanilla until creamy. Add the egg and mix until all ingredients are fully incorporated.

4. Add the dry ingredients to the butter mixture. Using a spatula, mix all the ingredients together, scraping down the sides of the bowl. Stir the chocolate chips into the dough.

5. Use the remaining 2 tablespoons of butter to coat a small cast-iron skillet. Add the cookie dough to the skillet, spreading it in an even layer.

6. Bake for 25 minutes or until the cookie begins to turn brown on top.

For the Sous Chef:

Start steps 1 and 2 while the chef begins mixing the wet ingredients in step 3. Then, jump ahead to step 5 to prepare the skillet.

3

Recipes for More: Easy, Practical Parties

Cooking together has not only brought us closer as a couple, but it also allows us to spend time with those we love. Whether we get the gang together for game night or host a party with a themed menu, we love to entertain. So much so, in fact, that we made a resolution this year to host a dinner party every month, drawing inspiration from different parts of the world.

The truth is that you don't need fancy china, matching flatware, or perfect décor to host a party. In fact, you don't even need enough chairs. You can always borrow chairs from the neighbors or throw some pillows on the floor around the coffee table.

No matter the occasion—a last-minute cocktail hour or hosting extended family for the holidays—you can use a few simple strategies to entertain with ease. This chapter introduces you to those ideas with menus for five easy parties, filled with doable menus that are delicious and feed a crowd. It's all aimed at spending less time stressing in the kitchen and more time enjoying the party.

No-Fuss Cocktail Party

A cocktail party can be as simple or complex as you like, but we think it is the perfect way to dip your toe into entertaining without making a big commitment. That is because there is no need for a full-course meal—all you need are a few hors d'oeuvres and some fun cocktails!

Let guests graze throughout the event, and have a few drink options. We recommend having a bottle of red wine and white wine open, a case of beer, and a few spirit options so everyone can sip on something they enjoy. Don't forget a sparkling water or mocktail option for those driving or declining for other reasons.

In this chapter, we offer two fun cocktail recommendations—Paloma Cocktails (page 130) and Bourbon & Peach Tea Punch (page 131)—along with boozy dessert Prosecco Ice Pops (page 132). We also curated some of our favorite small bites, most of which can be prepped in advance so you spend less time in the kitchen and more time at the party. Cheers!

BLUE CHEESE–STUFFED OLIVES	**122**
BACON-WRAPPED DATES	**123**
POTATO & CHORIZO BITES	**124**
BEEF WELLINGTON BITES	**126**
THE PERFECT GRAZING BOARD	**128**
PALOMA COCKTAILS	**130**
BOURBON & PEACH TEA PUNCH	**131**
PROSECCO ICE POPS	**132**

BLUE CHEESE-STUFFED OLIVES

SERVES 6 TO 8 | PREP TIME: 20 MINUTES

Gluten Free, Nut Free

Stuffed olives are perfect for a cocktail party because they serve double duty. Serve them with your cheese board or place them in a cute dish next to the bar. Guests can enjoy them as a snack while they graze or toss them into a martini for a classy cocktail. Either way, these olives are the perfect combination of briny and buttery. If blue cheese isn't your jam, don't worry—swap it out for Gorgonzola for a twist on this classic combination. Just be sure to choose large green olives so you can stuff them full of cheese.

¾ CUP GOOD QUALITY BLUE CHEESE

1 TABLESPOON HEAVY (WHIPPING) CREAM

CAYENNE PEPPER, FOR SEASONING (OPTIONAL)

24 LARGE GREEN OLIVES, PITTED

1. In a large bowl, combine the blue cheese, heavy cream, and a pinch of cayenne (if using). Using a handheld electric mixture, beat until fluffy.

2. Spoon the mixture into a pastry or plastic bag (and snip off a bottom corner). Pipe the mixture into each olive.

> **MAKE-AHEAD TIP:** Make these the day before, and refrigerate them in an airtight container.

BACON-WRAPPED DATES

SERVES 6 TO 8 | PREP TIME: 15 MINUTES | COOK TIME: 15 TO 18 MINUTES

Dairy Free, Gluten Free, Nut Free, One Pot

Simple finger foods are the key to an effortless cocktail party, and these Bacon-Wrapped Dates are just that. Despite only requiring two simple ingredients, they are always a big hit. The combination of salty and sweet means each bite is packed with flavor. If you want to get really fancy, offer a few different varieties. We recommend stuffing the dates with an almond, cheese, or both! In summer, try swapping the date with a pineapple chunk.

24 DATES, PITTED

12 BACON SLICES, HALVED WIDTHWISE

1. Preheat the oven to 400°F. Line a baking sheet with parchment paper and set aside.

2. Wrap each date with ½ slice of bacon, securing it with a toothpick where the bacon overlaps.

3. Place the wrapped dates on the prepared baking sheet and bake for 10 minutes. Remove the baking sheet from the oven and flip each date.

4. Bake for 5 to 8 minutes more, until golden brown and crispy. Remove from the oven and transfer the dates to a paper towel–lined plate.

> **PREP TIP:** The bacon should be cold when wrapping the dates. The warmer the bacon, the more difficult it is to handle.

POTATO & CHORIZO BITES

SERVES 6 TO 8 | PREP TIME: 10 MINUTES | COOK TIME: 40 MINUTES

Gluten Free, Nut Free

A riff on a twice-baked potato, these bites are a delicious addition to any cocktail party. We love that they are bite size but still filling, so you can enjoy another cocktail with something in your belly. The hollowed potatoes offer the perfect vessel for the spicy chorizo filling. You can also use this technique for a number of fillings. Swap the chorizo for bacon or choose a broccoli and cheese variation.

10 PETITE POTATOES, WASHED

SEA SALT

8 OUNCES SPICY CHORIZO, CASINGS REMOVED

¼ RED ONION, MINCED

1 GARLIC CLOVE, MINCED

½ CUP SOUR CREAM

HOT SAUCE, FOR SEASONING

FRESHLY GROUND BLACK PEPPER

2 SCALLIONS, THINLY SLICED

1. In a large stockpot, combine the potatoes with enough water to cover and season the water with salt. Bring to a boil over high heat, reduce the heat to medium, and simmer for 5 to 8 minutes, until fork-tender. Drain the potatoes and let them cool.

2. Meanwhile, preheat the oven to 375°F. Line a baking sheet with aluminum foil and a plate with paper towels and set aside.

3. In a medium cast-iron skillet over medium heat, cook the chorizo until browned and cooked through, breaking it up with a wooden spoon while cooking, about 5 minutes. Using a slotted spoon, transfer the chorizo to the prepared plate.

4. Return the skillet to medium-low heat, and add the red onion and garlic to the skillet. Sauté for 8 to 10 minutes, stirring frequently, until the onion is translucent.

5. Halve the potatoes. Using a spoon, hollow out some of the potato, about halfway, scooping the cooked flesh into a medium bowl.

6. Add the cooked chorizo, onion and garlic, sour cream, and a few dashes of hot sauce to the bowl. Season with salt and pepper. Gently stir to combine.

7. Fill the hollowed-out potatoes with the chorizo mixture and arrange the potatoes on the prepared baking sheet. Bake for 10 to 15 minutes, until golden brown.

8. Garnish with scallion.

BEEF WELLINGTON BITES

SERVES 6 TO 8 | PREP TIME: 15 MINUTES | COOK TIME: 35 MINUTES

Cozy Comforts, Nut Free

Although there is no need to serve a full meal at a cocktail party, we always make sure there are a few hearty options so our guests don't leave hungry. This recipe is a fun twist on the full-size classic. All the components and flavor of a traditional beef Wellington, from the tender beef to the buttery puff pastry, but prepared in a bite-size package. We promise your guests will be impressed!

1 TABLESPOON EXTRA-VIRGIN
OLIVE OIL

2 POUNDS BEEF TENDERLOIN,
TRIMMED AND CUT INTO
1-INCH CUBES

SEA SALT

FRESHLY GROUND
BLACK PEPPER

1 TABLESPOON
UNSALTED BUTTER

6 OUNCES BUTTON
MUSHROOMS, MINCED

2 SHALLOTS, MINCED

1½ TEASPOONS CHOPPED
FRESH THYME LEAVES

1½ TEASPOONS CHOPPED
FRESH ROSEMARY LEAVES

ALL-PURPOSE FLOUR,
FOR DUSTING

2 SHEETS FROZEN PUFF
PASTRY, THAWED

½ CUP PLUS 3 TABLESPOONS
DIJON MUSTARD

1 EGG, LIGHTLY BEATEN

1. Preheat the oven to 400°F. Line two baking sheets with aluminum foil and set aside.

2. In a medium cast-iron skillet over medium-high heat, heat olive oil.

3. Pat the meat dry with a paper towel and season all sides with salt and pepper. Place the meat in the skillet and cook until it is evenly browned on all sides, about 5 minutes total. Remove the meat from the skillet and wipe the skillet clean.

4. Return the skillet to medium heat and add the butter to melt. Add the mushrooms and shallots and sauté for 5 to 8 minutes, until tender.

5. Remove from the heat and add the thyme and rosemary. Season with salt and pepper and stir to combine.

6. Lightly flour a work surface and unfold the puff pastry on it. Roll each sheet into a large square, about ⅛ inch thick. Cut each piece into 16 squares.

7. Place one piece of meat onto each square and top with 1 tablespoon of the mushroom mixture and 1 teaspoon of mustard.

8. Fold the pastry edges over the meat, pinching the edges together to seal them.

9. Arrange the puff pastry bites on the prepared baking sheets and brush each with egg wash. Bake for 15 minutes or until golden brown.

PREP TIP: Save time by assembling the beef Wellington bites the night before, then pop them in the oven a few minutes before guests are expected to arrive.

THE PERFECT GRAZING BOARD

SERVES 6 TO 8 | PREP TIME: 20 MINUTES

Perhaps one of the biggest (and easiest!) entertaining trends is the grazing board. Say "so long" to individual appetizers, and embrace this oversized and overstuffed cheese and charcuterie board. The best part about this trend? There is no cooking necessary; just assemble and let guests help themselves. You don't even need to follow a specific recipe—just pick and choose (two or three options from each category) from the recommendations that follow, and arrange them all on a giant cutting board. If you don't have an oversized cutting board, arrange the items on multiple boards side by side. To ensure that guests dig in, make sure everything on the board is precut or sliced into one- or two-bite pieces. That way, they can try a little bit of everything.

	CHEESE	MEAT	DIPS	FRUITS AND VEGETABLES	BREAD AND CRACKERS	OTHER
WE LIKE:	Aged, hard, and semi-firm cheeses work best. We recommend crowd pleasers such as cheddar, Parmesan, and Manchego, along with a fancier option like Gouda or a Swiss style.	Opt for thinly sliced, well-marbled cured meats, such as prosciutto, capicola, and salami.	Keep things simple and reach for a few different premade dips, jams, and purées or make your own. We highly recommend our White Bean Hummus (page 57), Spinach Artichoke Dip (page 58), or creamy Tzatziki (page 184).	Choose bite-size seasonal fruits and vegetables to enjoy on their own or slice for dipping! Try red and green grapes, radishes, carrots, endive leaves, and cherry tomatoes.	Pick crunchy crackers and crusty bread that add a bit of texture to the selection. We like whole-wheat crackers, sliced baguette, or toasted sourdough bread.	Add a handful of roasted or candied nuts and a few pickled items such as cornichons or Blue Cheese–Stuffed Olives (page 122).
PREP:	Serve cheese with edible rinds in triangles, crumble hard cheeses, and cut other cheeses with round edges into half-moons.	Arrange smaller slices overlapping on the board or try rolling and folding larger slices for a unique presentation.	Spoon dips into bowls of varying colors and sizes and place on the board to add dimension.	Slice vegetables into different shapes for optimal dipping and nibbling. Arrange veggies around dips and place fruits that pair with cheese and meat together.	Swirl or stack the bread and crackers into remaining empty spaces on the board.	Fill in the remaining spaces with nuts and squeeze in an extra bowl or two filled with the pickled ingredients.

PREP TIP: The day before the cocktail party, slice the cheese, meats, and veggies, then prep any of the homemade dips. Refrigerate them in separate airtight containers. You can also get a head start by gathering the boards and bowls you will be using.

PALOMA COCKTAILS

SERVES 6 TO 8 | PREP TIME: 10 MINUTES, PLUS 1 HOUR TO CHILL

Dairy Free, Gluten Free, Nut Free, One Pot

The most important part of the cocktail party is, of course, the cocktails! Rather than outfitting a full bar, we recommend picking one or two signature cocktails that match the night's theme. This way, you can prep them in advance and spend your evening talking to guests rather than playing bartender. The Paloma is a tequila-based cocktail made with grapefruit and lime juices. What we love most is that this version makes a big batch that serves 6 to 8 people. Serve with a splash of sparkling water and a grapefruit wedge!

2⅔ CUPS FRESHLY SQUEEZED GRAPEFRUIT JUICE

1 CUP FRESHLY SQUEEZED LIME JUICE

1 CUP WATER

5 TABLESPOONS AGAVE NECTAR

2⅔ CUPS TEQUILA

½ TEASPOON SALT

SPARKLING WATER, FOR SERVING

GRAPEFRUIT WEDGES, FOR GARNISH

LIME WEDGES, FOR GARNISH

1. In a large pitcher, stir together the grapefruit juice, lime juice, water, and agave nectar. Chill for 1 hour.

2. Stir in the tequila and salt.

3. To serve, pour the cocktail over ice and top off with sparkling water.

4. Garnish with grapefruit and lime wedges.

BOURBON & PEACH TEA PUNCH

SERVES 6 TO 8 | PREP TIME: 10 MINUTES

Dairy Free, Gluten Free, Nut Free, One Pot

When picking the perfect cocktails for this menu, we wanted to choose two bright and bold cocktails that would be an excellent addition to any cocktail party, but that can also be enjoyed in a number of other settings. This punch is inspired by summer flavors and is the perfect recipe to enjoy out of large Mason jars on the porch. We love using frozen peaches instead of ice cubes to keep the cocktail cold without watering it down—plus, you get to eat the peaches at the end!

4 CUPS SWEETENED ICED TEA

3 CUPS BOURBON

2 CUPS PEACH NECTAR

1 CUP FRESHLY SQUEEZED LEMON JUICE

2 CUPS FROZEN PEACH SLICES

1. In a large pitcher, stir together the iced tea, bourbon, peach nectar, and lemon juice.

2. Stir in the peach slices and serve over ice.

PROSECCO ICE POPS

SERVES 8 | PREP TIME: 10 MINUTES, PLUS 8 HOURS TO FREEZE

Dairy Free, Gluten Free, Nut Free

No party is complete without dessert, but for a cocktail party we like to kick things up a notch with a boozy treat. Not only are these ice pops delicious, but they are also insanely cute! If you do not have ice pop molds, use paper or plastic cups. Fill them, then place a sheet of plastic wrap on top and gently poke a hole through the wrap with an ice-pop stick. Freeze for a few hours, then wiggle the pop out of the cup and enjoy. Ice cube trays work well, too. These ice pops can be made up to one week in advance. You can also swap out the fruit for whatever you have on hand.

1½ CUPS STRAWBERRIES

1½ CUPS CHOPPED MANGO

JUICE OF 1 LEMON

½ CUP SIMPLE SYRUP

2 BOTTLES PROSECCO

1. In a high-speed blender, combine the strawberries, mango, and lemon juice. Blend until smooth.

2. In a large bowl, combine the fruit purée, simple syrup, and one bottle of prosecco. Let stand until the bubbles from the prosecco subside.

3. Pour the mixture evenly into ice pop molds. Insert an ice pop stick into each mold. Freeze for 8 hours, or overnight.

4. To serve, fill a vessel with ice and arrange ice pops on top. Or place the pops upside down in cocktail glasses, and add a splash of prosecco to each glass.

> **PREP TIP**: To make your own simple syrup, combine equal parts (say, 1 cup each) sugar and water in a small saucepan over medium heat. Heat until the sugar dissolves. Cool and keep refrigerated for up to two weeks.

Birthday Brunch

In our house, we do birthdays in a big way, from long weekends away to surprising each other with visits from friends and family we haven't seen in a while. We love celebrating together and with those we love, especially over good food! Birthday brunch is one of our favorite ways to celebrate. Celebrate each other or someone special in your life with the following menu. To keep things simple and laid back, set up the food as a big buffet.

While the recipes in this chapter were chosen specifically for a birthday brunch, simply omit the Sprinkle-Loaded Waffles (page 141) and Chocolate Cake with Buttercream Frosting (page 142), and you can easily use this menu for Easter Brunch, Mother's Day, or just an excuse to get together with friends and family.

If you choose to celebrate birthdays with a dinner or cocktail party instead of brunch, mix and match recipes from the other menus throughout the book to make it your own!

We wish you a happy birthday!

MINI AVOCADO & RICOTTA TOASTS	**135**
SIMPLE FRUIT SALAD	**136**
COFFEE CAKE MUFFINS	**137**
EASY BACON & BROCCOLI STRATA	**138**
MIMOSA BAR	**139**
SPRINKLE-LOADED WAFFLES	**141**
CHOCOLATE CAKE WITH BUTTERCREAM FROSTING	**142**
PUMPKIN SPICE ICED COFFEE	**144**

MINI AVOCADO & RICOTTA TOASTS

SERVES 8 | PREP TIME: 15 MINUTES | COOK TIME: 5 MINUTES

Nut Free

These days, toast is a far cry from the boring white bread and butter we enjoyed as kids. Now it's all about a thick, crusty bread topped with avocado or ricotta and accoutrements. When adapting this trend for a crowd, we recommend doing this version of mini toasts with various toppings so everyone finds something to enjoy!

4 BREAD SLICES (WE RECOMMEND WHOLE-WHEAT SOURDOUGH)

1 RIPE AVOCADO, HALVED AND PITTED

1 TEASPOON FRESHLY SQUEEZED LEMON JUICE

SEA SALT

1 TEASPOON EXTRA-VIRGIN OLIVE OIL

RED PEPPER FLAKES, FOR SEASONING

1 RADISH, THINLY SLICED

1 TEASPOON PEPITAS

½ CUP FRESH RICOTTA

3 TABLESPOONS RASPBERRY JAM

3 TABLESPOONS STRAWBERRY JAM

1. In a toaster, toast the bread to your desired doneness and quarter each piece of toast.

2. Using a wide spoon, scoop the avocado halves from the peel into a small bowl. Add the lemon juice and ¼ teaspoon salt and mash until well combined.

3. Top half the toast pieces with the avocado mixture. Drizzle olive oil on top and sprinkle with red pepper flakes. Garnish with radish slices and pepitas.

4. In a medium bowl, using a handheld electric mixer, beat the ricotta with a pinch of salt until creamy.

5. Top the remaining 8 pieces of toast with the ricotta and add a dollop of raspberry or strawberry jam to each.

> **PREP TIP:** While you can easily beat the ricotta in advance and refrigerate it until you are ready to serve, we recommend making the avocado mixture right before guests arrive.

SIMPLE FRUIT SALAD

SERVES 8 | PREP TIME: 15 MINUTES

Dairy Free, Gluten Free, Nut Free

Fruit salad is a simple yet refreshing dish that is a staple of any brunch. The bright fruit is as delicious as it is beautiful—the perfect combination of sweet and tangy. While the ingredients listed produce a rainbow of colors perfect for a birthday brunch, you can customize the dish based on the event. Just pick the fruits that best match your color scheme. Serve it up in a big glass bowl, or layer it with yogurt for the ultimate parfait.

1 POUND FRESH STRAWBERRIES, WASHED, HULLED, AND SLICED

3 KIWI FRUITS, PEELED, HALVED, AND SLICED

2 MANGOS, PEELED AND DICED

10 OUNCES FRESH BLUEBERRIES, WASHED

1 CUP GREEN GRAPES, HALVED

1 (9-OUNCE) CAN PINEAPPLE CHUNKS, DRAINED, JUICE RESERVED

3 TABLESPOONS HONEY

1 TABLESPOON FRESHLY SQUEEZED LIME JUICE

1. In a large bowl, combine the strawberries, kiwi fruits, mangos, blueberries, grapes, and pineapple.

2. In a small bowl, stir together the honey, lime juice, and 1 tablespoon of reserved pineapple juice. Pour the honey mixture over the fruit and mix well.

> **PREP TIP:** This fruit salad can be made in advance using any in-season fruits you like (blackberries, pear, apple, orange slices, etc.); however, if you want to add banana slices, we recommend waiting to add them until just before serving. Also, be sure to mix the fruit with the juices at the bottom of the bowl again before serving.

COFFEE CAKE MUFFINS

SERVES 8 | PREP TIME: 20 MINUTES | COOK TIME: 25 MINUTES

Nut Free

This recipe is one of the biggest and best-kept secrets in Julien's family. When he was growing up, his mom always made a coffee cake for holiday brunches and birthday celebrations. Her coffee cake is beloved, but the truth is the base is made from a box mix! We're passing along this family secret here. We like to bake these as cupcakes so they are convenient for a crowd, but you can turn this into a round cake if you prefer—just follow the instructions on the box.

FOR THE CUPCAKES

1 BOX YELLOW CAKE MIX, AND THE INGREDIENTS NEEDED TO PREPARE IT ACCORDING TO THE PACKAGE DIRECTIONS (VEGETABLE OIL, WATER, AND EGGS)

FOR THE CRUMBLE TOPPING

4 CUPS ALL-PURPOSE FLOUR

1 CUP GRANULATED SUGAR

3 TABLESPOONS GROUND CINNAMON

2 CUPS (4 STICKS) UNSALTED BUTTER, MELTED

POWDERED SUGAR, FOR GARNISH

TO MAKE THE CUPCAKES

1. Preheat the oven to the temperature listed on the package directions, usually 350°F.

2. Prepare the boxed cake mix as cupcakes, per the package instructions, and bake as instructed until just cooked through. Remove them from the oven; leave the oven on.

TO MAKE THE CRUMBLE TOPPING

1. Meanwhile, in a large bowl, stir together the flour, sugar, and cinnamon.

2. Add the melted butter and stir until well combined and the mixture is a crumbly consistency. Spread the crumble topping on the cupcakes and bake for 4 to 5 minutes.

3. Remove and let cool completely. Using a fine-mesh sieve, dust with powdered sugar.

EASY BACON & BROCCOLI STRATA

SERVES 8 | PREP TIME: 10 MINUTES, PLUS 8 HOURS TO CHILL | COOK TIME: 1 HOUR

Cozy Comforts, Nut Free

This custardy, bready, cheesy breakfast casserole is one of our favorite things to make when entertaining for brunch. We love that you can assemble it the night before and pop it in the oven in the morning. What we love even more is that a breakfast strata is what we refer to as a "kitchen sink" recipe. Meaning it can have everything—but! Just follow the ratios below and bake a strata with whatever you have in the fridge. All you need is a combination of bread, milk, eggs, cheese, and any other mix-ins you want to include!

1 ITALIAN BREAD LOAF, CUT INTO 1-INCH CUBES

NONSTICK COOKING SPRAY, FOR PREPARING THE BAKING DISH

1 POUND SLICED BACON, COOKED AND CHOPPED

2 CUPS SHREDDED CHEDDAR CHEESE

1½ CUPS CHOPPED BROCCOLI

1 TABLESPOON DICED FRESH CHIVES

8 EGGS

2 CUPS WHOLE MILK

½ TEASPOON SEA SALT

½ TEASPOON FRESHLY GROUND BLACK PEPPER

1. Preheat the oven to 200°F. Line a baking sheet with aluminum foil.

2. Arrange the bread evenly on the baking sheet and bake for 5 to 10 minutes, until dried out.

3. Coat a 9-by-13-inch baking dish with cooking spray. Combine the bread, bacon, cheddar cheese, broccoli, and chives in the prepared dish.

4. In a medium bowl, whisk the eggs and milk. Season with the salt and pepper. Pour the egg mixture over the bread mixture in the baking dish, ensuring the bread is covered so it will soak in the egg mixture.

5. Cover the dish with aluminum foil and refrigerate overnight.

6. When ready to bake, preheat the oven to 350°F.

7. Bake the strata, covered, for 20 minutes then remove the foil and bake for 20 to 30 minutes more.

MIMOSA BAR

SERVES 8 | PREP TIME: 10 MINUTES

Dairy Free, Gluten Free, Nut Free

No brunch is complete without a mimosa! This mimosa bar is a more elegant take on ordinary punches usually served at brunch, and it's super easy to set up. All you need are a few different fruit juices and a couple bottles of Champagne or prosecco. Serve sliced fruit alongside for garnish, and encourage your guests to experiment with different combinations. Set out champagne flutes for guests to serve themselves.

2 BOTTLES DRY CHAMPAGNE, PROSECCO, OR OTHER SPARKLING WINE, CHILLED, OPENED, AND ON ICE TO KEEP COLD

3 CUPS FRESHLY SQUEEZED ORANGE JUICE

3 CUPS PINEAPPLE JUICE

3 CUPS PEACH PURÉE

FRESH RASPBERRIES, BLUEBERRIES, OR PEACH SLICES, FOR GARNISH

1. Pour the orange juice, pineapple juice, and peach purée into three separate pitchers

2. To serve, fill each flute about halfway, or a bit less, with fruit juice of choice. Top off with bubbles. Add a fruit garnish to finish.

SPRINKLE-LOADED WAFFLES

SERVES 6 | PREP TIME: 5 MINUTES | COOK TIME: 5 MINUTES

Cozy Comforts, Date Night, Meatless Monday, Nut Free, Weeknight

Waffles are a classic breakfast and brunch staple—crisp and golden on the outside, light and fluffy on the inside. This version is perfect for a birthday celebration because they are loaded with rainbow sprinkles! Make a batch of waffles in advance, and then toast them when guests arrive. Top with fresh fruit and maple syrup, or truly channel dessert for breakfast with a dollop of whipped cream.

2 EGGS

2 CUPS ALL-PURPOSE FLOUR

1¾ CUPS MILK

½ CUP VEGETABLE OIL

1 TABLESPOON PLUS
1 TEASPOON BAKING POWDER

1 TABLESPOON SUGAR

¼ TEASPOON SALT

1 TEASPOON
VANILLA EXTRACT

½ CUP RAINBOW SPRINKLES

NONSTICK COOKING SPRAY,
FOR PREPARING THE
WAFFLE IRON

1. Preheat a stovetop waffle iron over medium-high heat, or preheat an electric waffle iron according to the manufacturer's instructions.

2. In a large bowl, whisk the eggs until fluffy. Add the flour, milk, vegetable oil, baking powder, sugar, and salt and whisk until smooth.

3. Add the vanilla and sprinkles and gently stir to fold in.

4. Spray the waffle iron on both sides with cooking spray. Use a ladle to spoon the batter onto the iron.

5. Cook for 2 minutes, flip the iron, and cook for 2 to 3 minutes more (cook for 4 to 5 minutes in an electric waffle iron, but no need to flip!). Carefully remove the waffles and serve with maple syrup, whipped cream, or other desired toppings.

CHOCOLATE CAKE WITH BUTTERCREAM FROSTING

SERVES 8 TO 10 | PREP TIME: 20 MINUTES | COOK TIME: 35 MINUTES
Nut Free

A birthday celebration is not complete without a cake. This decadent chocolate cake is rich and moist with the perfect tender crumb. Paired with a luxurious buttercream frosting, it is irresistible. To ensure that the cake is as beautiful as it is tasty, spread a thin layer of frosting, called a "crumb coat," all over the cake before fully frosting it. This helps smooth out the crumbs to prepare for the final coating. Add a few candles, and get ready to sing!

FOR THE CHOCOLATE CAKE

½ CUP (1 STICK) UNSALTED BUTTER, MELTED, PLUS MORE FOR PREPARING THE CAKE PANS

2 CUPS SUGAR

2 CUPS ALL-PURPOSE FLOUR

¾ CUP UNSWEETENED COCOA POWDER

1½ TEASPOONS BAKING POWDER

1½ TEASPOONS BAKING SODA

1 TEASPOON SALT

2 EGGS

1 CUP BUTTERMILK

2 TABLESPOONS VANILLA EXTRACT

1 CUP BOILING WATER

FOR THE BUTTERCREAM FROSTING

1 CUP (2 STICKS) UNSALTED BUTTER, AT ROOM TEMPERATURE

1 CUP UNSWEETENED COCOA POWDER

2½ CUPS POWDERED SUGAR

½ CUP WHOLE MILK

To make the chocolate cake

1. Preheat the oven to 350°F. Lightly coat two 9-inch cake pans with butter.

2. In a large bowl, stir together the sugar, flour, cocoa powder, baking powder, baking soda, and salt.

3. In a small bowl, whisk together the eggs, buttermilk, ½ cup melted butter, and vanilla until well combined.

4. Add the wet ingredients to the flour mixture and mix well. Add the boiling water and mix until well combined.

5. Evenly divide the batter between the prepared cake pans. Bake on the middle rack for 30 to 35 minutes, until a toothpick inserted into the center comes out clean. Cool completely on a wire rack.

To make the buttercream frosting

1. Meanwhile, in a large bowl, using a handheld electric mixer, beat the butter on medium speed.

2. Switch to low speed and slowly add the cocoa powder, mixing until fully incorporated. Slowly add the powdered sugar and milk, mixing on medium speed for 3 to 5 minutes, until light and fluffy.

3. Once the cake is completely cooled, frost and assemble the cake.

PUMPKIN SPICE ICED COFFEE

SERVES 6 | PREP TIME: 15 MINUTES

Cozy Comforts, Date Night, Gluten Free, Meatless Monday, Weeknight

When you are hosting a birthday brunch, the coffee is just as important as the booze. While it is typical to have a carafe of hot coffee, why not switch things up with a pitcher of Pumpkin Spice Iced Coffee as well? You don't need to stop at the local chain to get this seasonal favorite flavor.

Our tip to keep the coffee cold throughout the event without getting watered down? Freeze coffee in an ice cube tray the night before to create iced-coffee cubes, and add them to the pitcher.

6 CUPS BREWED COFFEE

1½ TEASPOONS GROUND CINNAMON

1 TEASPOON GROUND GINGER

¼ TEASPOON GROUND ALLSPICE

¼ TEASPOON GROUND CLOVES

¼ TEASPOON GROUND NUTMEG

3 CUPS MILK OF CHOICE

1. While the coffee is still warm, stir in the cinnamon, ginger, allspice, cloves, and nutmeg.

2. Once the coffee has cooled, pour it into a large pitcher with the milk. Stir to combine, and pour over ice to serve.

SWAP IT OUT: If you are serving the coffee to a crowd with different milk preferences, you can have each guest make their own instead of mixing it in a pitcher.

Weekend BBQ

A backyard barbecue is one of our favorite ways to spend a summer afternoon. Whether you have a big backyard or a little deck in the middle of the city, put a Mason jar full of flowers on the table and string up some twinkle lights—then let the food be the star of the show.

There is nothing better than grilling burgers and spending time in the sun, followed by Peanut Butter Cup S'mores (page 154) on a warm summer night under the stars. Dining alfresco doesn't have to be fancy; it just has to be fun! These recipes can be used for any summer event, including Memorial Day, Fourth of July, and Labor Day.

DEVILED EGGS	146
CARAMELIZED ONION DIP	147
WATERMELON & FETA SALAD	148
ELOTE CORN SALAD	149
HOMEMADE BURGER BAR	150
GOCHUJANG BBQ CHICKEN	152
PEANUT BUTTER CUP S'MORES	154
ADULT LEMONADE	155

DEVILED EGGS

SERVES 6 | PREP TIME: 20 MINUTES | COOK TIME: 15 MINUTES

Cozy Comforts, Date Night, Dairy Free, Gluten Free, Meatless Monday, Nut Free, Weeknight

Deviled eggs are perfect for any party or gathering because they are simple to prepare and easy to enjoy as a finger food.

9 EGGS

½ CUP MAYONNAISE

2 TEASPOONS YELLOW MUSTARD

1 TEASPOON WHITE VINEGAR

¼ TEASPOON SALT

FRESHLY GROUND BLACK PEPPER

PAPRIKA, FOR GARNISH

1. Place the eggs in a single layer in a pot, and add enough cool water to cover them by 1 inch. Cover the pot, place it on the stovetop, turn the heat to high, and let the water come to a boil.

2. Turn the heat under the pot to medium-high, cover the pot, and boil the eggs for 8 minutes. Using a slotted spoon, carefully remove the eggs and rinse them under cold water for 1 minute.

3. Carefully remove the shells by peeling them under cool running water. Dry with a paper towel.

4. Halve the eggs lengthwise and scoop the yolks into a small bowl. Place the egg whites on a plate or serving platter.

5. Use a fork to crumble the yolks. Add the mayonnaise, mustard, vinegar, salt, and pepper; stir to combine.

6. Place a dollop of the yolk mixture into each egg white half. Garnish with a sprinkle of paprika.

> **KITCHEN HACK:** Boil the eggs in advance, and leave them in their shells in the refrigerator for up to five days.

CARAMELIZED ONION DIP

SERVES 6 | PREP TIME: 15 MINUTES | COOK TIME: 25 MINUTES

Cozy Comforts, Meatless Monday, Nut Free

One of the most basic staples for any backyard barbecue is chips and dip. Instead of reaching for the onion soup pack, step up your game with this homemade version. The caramelized onions pack a ton of flavor, while the combination of sour cream and cream cheese makes this dip smooth and delicious. Serve it with your favorite potato chips and fresh veggies for the perfect appetizer.

2 TABLESPOONS UNSALTED BUTTER

3 ONIONS, THINLY SLICED

2 TABLESPOONS WHITE WINE, DIVIDED

1½ CUPS SOUR CREAM, AT ROOM TEMPERATURE

1 (8-OUNCE) PACKAGE CREAM CHEESE, AT ROOM TEMPERATURE

½ TEASPOON DRIED PARSLEY

½ TEASPOON ONION POWDER

½ TEASPOON SOY SAUCE

SEA SALT

FRESHLY GROUND BLACK PEPPER

1. In a large skillet over medium heat, melt the butter. Add the onions and sauté for 15 minutes, stirring every so often.

2. Stir in 1 tablespoon of wine and cook until the liquid evaporates. Repeat with the remaining 1 tablespoon of wine. Once all the liquid has evaporated, remove the skillet from the heat and let cool slightly.

3. Place the onions on a cutting board and chop them coarsely.

4. In a large bowl, stir together the sour cream, cream cheese, parsley, onion powder, and soy sauce until fully combined. Fold in the onions and season with salt and pepper.

WATERMELON & FETA SALAD

SERVES 6 | PREP TIME: 15 MINUTES

Date Night, Gluten Free, Meatless Monday, Nut Free, Weeknight

There are some people out there who believe a salad has to have lettuce, macaroni, or potato in it to be considered a "salad." We are not in that camp! Cool, crisp watermelon meets salty feta and a citrusy dressing in this vibrant side salad. If you're in a time crunch, pick up some cut melon from your neighborhood market, and you can have this ready to go in just 5 minutes.

1 (6-POUND) SEEDLESS
WATERMELON, CHILLED

3 TABLESPOONS
EXTRA-VIRGIN OLIVE OIL

JUICE OF 2 LIMES

1 TEASPOON SALT

½ TEASPOON FRESHLY
GROUND BLACK PEPPER

¾ CUP FRESH MINT
LEAVES, CHOPPED

1 CUP CRUMBLED
FETA CHEESE

1. Cut the watermelon flesh from the rind, chop it into cubes, and place it in a colander in the sink to drain.

2. In a small bowl, whisk the olive oil, lime juice, salt, and pepper.

3. Pour the watermelon cubes into a large serving bowl. Add the dressing and mint; gently toss to coat.

4. Add the crumbled feta cheese and gently stir to incorporate.

> **PREP TIP:** Due to the water content of the watermelon, we do not recommend preparing this too far in advance of serving.

ELOTE CORN SALAD

SERVES 6 | PREP TIME: 5 MINUTES, PLUS 15 MINUTES TO COOL |
COOK TIME: 20 MINUTES

Cozy Comforts, Date Night, Gluten Free, Meatless Monday, Nut Free, Weeknight

Our last apartment was in an eclectic, bustling neighborhood with some of the best and most popular restaurants in Boston. One restaurant in particular was only a half block up the street and was notoriously busy every night of the week—they don't take reservations, so if you didn't show up 20 minutes before opening, you were almost always guaranteed a wait! They have some of the best tapas in the city, including grilled street corn topped with a zesty mayonnaise sauce. We wanted to recreate the flavor in a crowd-friendly format: Enter this salad, where we cut the corn off the cob to make eating (and cleaning up) a breeze!

6 EARS CORN, SHUCKED, WITH AS MUCH SILK REMOVED AS POSSIBLE

3 TABLESPOONS UNSALTED BUTTER, CUT INTO 6 PIECES

⅓ CUP MAYONNAISE

1 TEASPOON CHILI POWDER

½ TEASPOON CAYENNE PEPPER

½ TEASPOON ONION POWDER

½ TEASPOON GARLIC POWDER

⅓ CUP FRESH CILANTRO LEAVES, CHOPPED

JUICE OF ½ LIME

½ CUP CRUMBLED COTIJA CHEESE

SEA SALT

FRESHLY GROUND BLACK PEPPER

1. Preheat a grill or a grill pan over medium heat.

2. Wrap each ear of corn in a piece of aluminum foil, with one piece of butter in each packet. Grill for 7 minutes, turn, and grill for 7 minutes more.

3. Carefully remove the ears from the foil and place them directly onto the grill to char some of the kernels slightly, about 2 minutes. Remove and set aside to cool for about 15 minutes.

4. In a medium bowl, stir together the mayonnaise, chili powder, cayenne, onion powder, garlic powder, cilantro, and lime juice until well mixed.

5. Once the corn has cooled, cut the kernels from the cob and place in a large bowl. Add the mayonnaise mixture and stir to combine. Top with the Cotija cheese, season with salt and pepper, and mix to combine.

HOMEMADE BURGER BAR

SERVES 6 | PREP TIME: 20 MINUTES | COOK TIME: 10 MINUTES

Cozy Comforts, Date Night, Nut Free, Weeknight

Burgers are the quintessential food of any barbecue day. With toppings and condiments galore, you can truly customize them any way imaginable. Offered here are what we consider our burger essentials—plus a "secret sauce" that will give a tangy kick to your burgers! Giving guests the chance to build their own burgers makes sure everyone gets exactly what they crave.

FOR THE BURGERS

3 POUNDS GROUND BEEF (WE RECOMMEND GROUND CHUCK, 80% TO 85% LEAN)

SEA SALT

FRESHLY GROUND BLACK PEPPER

FOR THE BURGER SAUCE

½ CUP MAYONNAISE

2 TABLESPOONS FRENCH DRESSING

1 TABLESPOON SWEET

PICKLE RELISH

1 TABLESPOON FINELY MINCED WHITE ONION

1 TEASPOON WHITE VINEGAR

1 TEASPOON SUGAR

SEA SALT, TO TASTE

FOR SERVING (ALL OPTIONAL)

3 SLICES AMERICAN CHEESE

3 SLICES CHEDDAR CHEESE

3 SLICES PEPPER JACK CHEESE

1 TOMATO, SLICED

9 TO 12 LEAVES BOSTON LETTUCE

1 RED ONION, SLICED

PICKLE SLICES

KETCHUP

MUSTARD

MAYONNAISE

SWEET PICKLE RELISH

6 HAMBURGER BUNS

TO MAKE THE BURGERS

1. Preheat a grill or a grill pan over high heat.

2. Divide the meat into 6 equal portions. Using your hands, form each portion into a burger that is about ¾ inch thick. With your thumb, create an indentation in the center of each patty. Season both sides of each patty with salt and pepper.

3. Place the burgers on the grill and cook for 3 to 4 minutes. Flip and cook for 5 to 6 minutes more to achieve medium doneness. Adjust your cooking time "after the flip" depending on your desired degree of doneness.

To make the burger sauce

While the burgers cook, make the sauce. In a small bowl, combine the mayonnaise, French dressing, relish, onion, vinegar, and sugar and season with salt. Whisk to blend the ingredients.

To prepare the toppings and serve

1. Layer the cheeses and vegetable toppings on plates or platters. Serve the burger sauce and other condiments in small bowls with spoons so your guests can easily spread their favorites on their burgers. Leave the hamburger buns on a separate plate or platter so they don't absorb any moisture from the toppings.

2. Serve the burgers on a separate plate or platter alongside the toppings, condiments, and buns.

> **PREP TIP:** The beauty of a DIY burger bar is that everyone can customize their burger. Offer big lettuce leaves for those who are gluten free, or pick up some plant-based veggie burgers for vegetarian and vegan friends.

GOCHUJANG BBQ CHICKEN

SERVES 6 | PREP TIME: 5 MINUTES | COOK TIME: 30 MINUTES

Cozy Comforts, Dairy Free, Date Night, Nut Free

Gochujang is a chili paste condiment originating from Korea. The spicy yet sweet flavor makes it a great substitute for the "traditional" barbecue sauce taste everyone knows. It's delicious on ribs or steak, but here we pair it with chicken to give your barbecue guests something new to try.

3 YELLOW ONIONS, COARSELY CHOPPED

6 GARLIC CLOVES, MINCED

¾ CUP SOY SAUCE

¾ CUP GOCHUJANG

6 TABLESPOONS SESAME OIL

3 TABLESPOONS HONEY

2 TABLESPOONS PACKED LIGHT BROWN SUGAR

1 TEASPOON RICE VINEGAR

5 POUNDS CHICKEN DRUMSTICKS AND BONE-IN CHICKEN THIGHS

1. Preheat a grill or a grill pan over medium heat.

2. In a medium bowl, combine the onions, garlic, soy sauce, gochujang, sesame oil, honey, brown sugar, and vinegar. Whisk to blend.

3. Heat a medium saucepan over medium-high heat. Add the sauce to the pan and bring to a boil, stirring occasionally. Once the sauce boils, remove it from the heat and set aside.

4. Meanwhile, place the chicken on the grill, skin-side up, and cook for 20 minutes.

5. Baste the chicken with the sauce, flip, and cook for 3 minutes more.

6. Baste and flip again, cooking for 3 minutes more.

> **SWAP IT OUT:** You can also make this with boneless chicken breasts or thighs, but pay careful attention to the cooking time so you don't dry out the chicken.

PEANUT BUTTER CUP S'MORES

SERVES 6 | PREP TIME: 5 MINUTES | COOK TIME: 5 MINUTES

Cozy Comforts, Meatless Monday, One Pot, Weeknight

Take your s'mores game to the next level by swapping out the traditional chocolate bar for a peanut butter cup. What you'll end up with is something like a Fluffernutter sandwich and a s'more put together! Because not everyone has access to a fire pit to roast marshmallows on sticks, we wanted to share how you can get this taste of summer right on the grill or from the oven.

6 GRAHAM CRACKERS, BROKEN INTO SQUARE HALVES

6 REGULAR-SIZE PEANUT BUTTER CUPS

12 LARGE MARSHMALLOWS

1. Preheat a grill to medium heat, or preheat the oven to 450°F.

2. Cut six squares of aluminum foil. Place 1 graham cracker square in the center of each piece of foil. Layer on 1 peanut butter cup and 2 marshmallows. Top each with a graham cracker square.

3. Fold the foil up around the s'mores, and seal to create packets.

4. Grill or bake the foil packets for 4 to 5 minutes.

> **KITCHEN HACK:** These s'mores are easy to prepare in advance; just throw them on the grill or in the oven when you are ready for dessert!

ADULT LEMONADE

SERVES 6 | PREP TIME: 15 MINUTES, PLUS REFRIGERATION TIME

Cozy Comforts, Dairy Free, Date Night, Gluten Free, Meatless Monday, Nut Free, Weeknight

There's something nostalgic about a refreshing glass of lemonade on a hot summer day. Here, we've brought that flavor into an easy cocktail you can sip on outside or in. If you have young ones joining your barbecue, just leave the vodka separate and you'll have a delicious nonalcoholic lemonade for everyone to enjoy.

2 CUPS SUGAR

5 CUPS WATER, DIVIDED

ZEST OF 1 LEMON

1¾ CUPS FRESHLY SQUEEZED LEMON JUICE

1 CUP VODKA

6 ROSEMARY SPRIGS

1. In a large saucepan over medium heat, combine the sugar, 1 cup of water, and lemon zest. Cook for about 5 minutes, until the sugar dissolves.

2. Remove the pan from the heat and stir in the lemon juice and remaining 4 cups of water. Pour into a pitcher and refrigerate until chilled.

3. Once chilled, stir the vodka into the lemonade. Pour into ice-filled glasses and garnish each with a rosemary sprig.

> **SWAP IT OUT:** Change out the vodka for white rum for a different take on spiked lemonade.

Doable Dinner Party

So many people find hosting stressful, but it doesn't have to be. The key to a "doable" dinner party is early menu planning and prepping, as well as ensuring your kitchen is set up for success (pro tip: Make sure the dishwasher is empty). Most importantly, embrace a fun and relaxed atmosphere to keep you and your guests at ease. Master one menu, and then try another to build confidence as you go.

If you don't feel ready, or don't have the space to host a crowd, keep things simple by inviting just one other couple. There is nothing wrong with an intimate dinner party—in fact, we would be remiss to write a cookbook without mentioning our forever dinner dates, Alex and Maddison. Every week, we trade off cooking and hosting. Some weeks we have a four-course menu with a planned theme, and other weeks we just enjoy a big pot of pasta and sauce and a bottle of wine.

This menu is based on the first four-person dinner party we hosted after we got married in Italy. We were inspired by the amazing flavors we encountered while traveling from Tuscany to the coast. We hope you make amazing memories cooking together and enjoying these recipes with people you love. Buon appetito!

CAPRESE SALAD SKEWERS	157
ITALIAN CHEESE & CHARCUTERIE BOARD	158
APEROL SPRITZ	160
GRILLED ZUCCHINI WITH LEMON ZEST	161
GARLIC SAUTÉED BROCCOLI RABE	162
TROFIE AL PESTO	163
CHICKEN SALTIMBOCCA	164
SIMPLE TIRAMISU	166

CAPRESE SALAD SKEWERS

MAKES 15 SKEWERS | PREP TIME: 10 MINUTES

Cozy Comforts, Date Night, Gluten Free, Meatless Monday, Nut Free, One Pot, Weeknight

This is one of the easiest party starters, with the colors of the Italian flag in every bite. These mini-skewers pair the brightness of fresh cherry tomatoes with the creaminess of mozzarella cheese and the aroma of basil. Drizzled in olive oil and balsamic vinegar, these are sure to impress (and disappear quickly)!

15 CHERRY TOMATOES, HALVED

15 FRESH BASIL LEAVES

15 MOZZARELLA BOCCONCINI ("SMALL BALLS")

2 TABLESPOONS EXTRA-VIRGIN OLIVE OIL

2 TABLESPOONS BALSAMIC VINEGAR

SEA SALT

FRESHLY GROUND BLACK PEPPER

1. Thread a cherry tomato half, a folded basil leaf, one bocconcini, and another tomato half onto a toothpick. Repeat with the remaining tomatoes, basil, and bocconcini. Place in a single layer on a serving plate.

2. Lightly drizzle the olive oil and vinegar over the skewers and season with salt and pepper.

ITALIAN CHEESE & CHARCUTERIE BOARD

SERVES 6 | PREP TIME: 15 MINUTES

Cozy Comforts, Date Night, Nut Free, Weeknight

One of the best things about a cheese and charcuterie board is that there's no cooking required, making this a great dish to kick off your Doable Dinner Party. An Italian twist on our Perfect Grazing Board (page 128), we use the same principles to build this board but focus on items from Italy. Because this will be eaten alongside some larger dishes, we kept it simple so your guests will have plenty of room left for the other parts of the meal to follow!

4 OUNCES PROSCIUTTO DI PARMA

4 OUNCES SPECK

4 OUNCES SALAMI

1 (4-OUNCE) PIECE PARMIGIANO-REGGIANO CHEESE

1 (4-OUNCE) PIECE PROVOLONE CHEESE

1 (4-OUNCE) PIECE RICOTTA SALATA CHEESE

1 LOAF CRUSTY ITALIAN BREAD, SLICED

8 TO 10 CRUNCHY ITALIAN BREADSTICKS

½ CUP MARINATED MIXED OLIVES

¼ CUP MARINATED ROASTED RED PEPPERS

¼ CUP EXTRA-VIRGIN OLIVE OIL

SEA SALT

FRESHLY GROUND BLACK PEPPER

1. Arrange the prosciutto, speck, salami, Parmigiano-Reggiano, provolone, ricotta salata, and bread slices on a large board, starting at the center of the board and working your way out.

2. Place the olives and roasted red peppers in separate small dishes, and nestle them onto the board among the meat and cheese.

3. Pour the olive oil into a small dish and season with salt and pepper. Add the dish to the board and serve.

FOR TWO/FOR A CROWD: A cheese and charcuterie board is easy to scale up or down, depending on the number of people you are serving. In general, you can assume 2 ounces of meat per person and 2 ounces of cheese per person if you are going to be serving other food alongside the board.

APEROL SPRITZ

SERVES 6 | PREP TIME: 5 MINUTES

Cozy Comforts, Dairy Free, Date Night, Gluten Free, Meatless Monday, Nut Free, One Pot, Weeknight

When hosting an Italian-themed dinner party, we're sure your mind may go directly to picking a bottle of wine (or a few). While we definitely support that, we also want to share a recipe for one of our favorite warm-weather Italian drinks—a classic Aperol Spritz. Often, you'll find this cocktail served in a big wine glass, but you can get creative. Just make sure to serve it over plenty of ice and top with an orange slice! It's a great pre-dinner aperitif before you crack open the bottle of red with the meal.

4½ CUPS PROSECCO (ABOUT 1½ BOTTLES)

3 CUPS APEROL

1½ CUPS CLUB SODA

1 ORANGE, SLICED

1. In a large pitcher, combine the prosecco, Aperol, and club soda. Stir until well mixed.

2. Pour into six ice-filled glasses. Garnish each glass with an orange slice.

GRILLED ZUCCHINI WITH LEMON ZEST

SERVES 6 | PREP TIME: 20 MINUTES | COOK TIME: 20 MINUTES

Cozy Comforts, Dairy Free, Date Night, Gluten Free, Meatless Monday, Nut Free, Weeknight

Zucchini is one of our shared favorite vegetables, so we knew we wanted to include a recipe in this dinner party! We like to prepare it in various ways, but as soon as summer starts we are constantly tossing it on the grill. Here, we keep it simple and fresh with a lemon zest marinade, and it works great on either a traditional grill or a grill pan on the stovetop.

4 MEDIUM ZUCCHINI, ENDS TRIMMED, QUARTERED LENGTHWISE

¼ CUP EXTRA-VIRGIN OLIVE OIL

ZEST AND JUICE OF 2 LEMONS, ZEST DIVIDED

SEA SALT

FRESHLY GROUND BLACK PEPPER

1. Heat a grill or grill pan over medium heat.

2. Place the zucchini quarters in a baking dish. Drizzle with the olive oil and lemon juice and season with salt and pepper. Sprinkle on half of the lemon zest and use tongs to move the zucchini spears around so they are evenly coated. Cover the dish and let the zucchini marinate for 15 minutes.

3. Transfer the zucchini onto the grill or place in the grill pan in a single layer. Cook for 5 to 6 minutes, then flip turn them to another side. Continue to cook and turn until all sides have been grilled.

4. While the zucchini cooks, in a small bowl, combine the remaining lemon zest with 2 teaspoons of salt. Sprinkle the lemon salt over the grilled zucchini and serve.

> **SWAP IT OUT:** Is your local market out of zucchini? Try asparagus; its flavor pairs perfectly with the lemon and salt notes of this dish.

GARLIC SAUTÉED BROCCOLI RABE

SERVES 6 | PREP TIME: 5 MINUTES | COOK TIME: 20 MINUTES

Cozy Comforts, Dairy Free, Date Night, Gluten Free, Meatless Monday, Nut Free, One Pot, Weeknight

Broccoli rabe, or rapini *in Italian, is a leafy green with small clusters of green buds that look like broccoli (the inspiration for the name). If you've never had it, it has a nutty and slightly bitter taste similar to mustard greens. We love the texture this brings to the table, especially with the crispy browned garlic added.*

2 BUNCHES BROCCOLI RABE, ENDS TRIMMED, CHOPPED

3 TABLESPOONS EXTRA-VIRGIN OLIVE OIL

5 GARLIC CLOVES, THINLY SLICED

SEA SALT

FRESHLY GROUND BLACK PEPPER

1. Rinse the broccoli rabe well under cold water and let drain fully.

2. In a large pot over low heat, heat the olive oil. Add the garlic and cook, stirring occasionally, for 5 minutes or until browned. Using a slotted spoon, remove the garlic from the oil and set aside.

3. Add the broccoli rabe to the oil and season with salt and pepper. Cover the pot and cook over low heat for 10 minutes, stirring occasionally, until the stalks are tender.

4. Add the garlic back into the broccoli rabe and stir to distribute throughout.

TROFIE AL PESTO

SERVES 6 | PREP TIME: 5 MINUTES | COOK TIME: 10 MINUTES

Cozy Comforts, Meatless Monday, One Pot, Weeknight

Our first trip to Italy together did not start off as relaxing as it should have. We booked a package on a popular travel website that included our hotel, flights, and rental car, and we were so excited to explore the Cinque Terre region. Little did we know that the airport closest to our final destination was super small and located right on the Mediterranean— meaning that when our tiny plane tried to land (three times) on a windy day, it couldn't! We were diverted several hours away to Torino, a city in northern Italy, and then shuttled to the original airport where we picked up our rental car. Two hours and a windy mountainside road later, we arrived in Portovenere almost a full 12 hours later than expected. Fortunately, everything went up from here, and our first meal in this beautiful town was this traditional Ligurian dish. The short, thin, twisted shape of the trofie pasta is a great vessel for an herby pesto sauce, and this has remained one of our favorite pastas since that trip.

1 POUND DRY TROFIE PASTA

½ CUP 5-INGREDIENT PESTO (PAGE 185)

1. Bring a large pot of water to a boil over high heat. Cook the pasta according to the package directions until it is al dente.

2. Drain the pasta, reserving 1 cup of the pasta water.

3. Return the pasta to the pot and stir in the pesto. A little at a time, add the reserved pasta water to help create a light sauce to coat the pasta.

> **SWAP IT OUT:** Trofie is a traditional pasta from the Liguria region of Italy, so if you don't have a great Italian market nearby, it may be a bit hard to find. If you need to use another pasta, we recommend fusilli, gemelli, or anything with "twists."

CHICKEN SALTIMBOCCA

SERVES 6 | PREP TIME: 1 HOUR 15 MINUTES | COOK TIME: 10 MINUTES

Cozy Comforts, Date Night, Gluten Free, Nut Free

The word saltimbocca *in Italian loosely translates to "jumps in the mouth." With the saltiness of the prosciutto and the crispy earthiness of the sage, you'll understand the translation with your first bite! While you have to plan a bit in advance to let the flavors of the garlic and sage infuse into the chicken, you can start this first and then prepare the appetizers and veggies in this menu while this sits and builds flavor.*

1½ POUNDS BONELESS, SKINLESS CHICKEN BREAST, CUT INTO 6 PIECES

SEA SALT

FRESHLY GROUND BLACK PEPPER

3 GARLIC CLOVES, PEELED

1 TABLESPOON CHOPPED FRESH SAGE, PLUS 20 TO 25 WHOLE FRESH SAGE LEAVES

4 TABLESPOONS EXTRA-VIRGIN OLIVE OIL, DIVIDED

6 SLICES PROSCIUTTO DI PARMA

6 SLICES MOZZARELLA CHEESE

1. Cover a clean work surface with parchment paper and place the chicken on it. Use a meat mallet or heavy pan to pound the chicken until it has flattened slightly. Season both sides of each piece with salt and pepper.

2. Use the flat end of a large knife to crush the garlic cloves into a paste. Rub the garlic paste, chopped sage, and 1 tablespoon of olive oil onto the chicken. Cover and let sit at room temperature for 1 hour.

3. In a large skillet over medium heat, heat the remaining 3 tablespoons of olive oil. Once the oil is hot, add the whole sage leaves and fry them for 30 seconds. Using a slotted spoon, remove them from the skillet and place them on a paper towel to drain, reserving the oil in the skillet.

4. Preheat the broiler.

5. Place the chicken into the skillet and cook for 2 minutes per side, until they begin to turn brown. Transfer the chicken to a baking sheet or dish in a single layer.

6. Layer two of the sage leaves, one slice of prosciutto, and one slice of mozzarella cheese on top of each piece of chicken.

7. Broil for 3 minutes or until the cheese is melted and bubbling. Serve with the remaining sage leaves as a garnish.

KITCHEN HACK: You can prepare the chicken in steps 1 and 2 several hours before cooking. Instead of leaving the chicken to marinate at room temperature for 1 hour, cover and refrigerate it until you're ready to proceed with the recipe.

SIMPLE TIRAMISU

SERVES 6 | PREP TIME: 15 MINUTES, PLUS 1 HOUR TO CHILL

Cozy Comforts, Date Night, Meatless Monday, Nut Free, Weeknight

Tiramisu is a texture and flavor explosion: You get the juxtaposition of a cakey bite and the soft mascarpone cheese mixture as well as the sweetness of sugar combined with the slight bitterness of coffee and cocoa powder. Somehow all these opposites attract and create an almost indescribable taste that can be found at Italian restaurants all over the U.S. (and Italy, of course)—and now in your own kitchen.

3 EGG YOLKS

¼ CUP SUGAR

2 TEASPOONS VANILLA EXTRACT

1½ CUPS MASCARPONE CHEESE

1½ CUPS BREWED COFFEE, COOLED

24 LADYFINGER COOKIES

COCOA POWDER, FOR GARNISH

1. In a medium bowl, whisk together the egg yolks, sugar, and vanilla until smooth. Using a spatula, fold in the mascarpone cheese.

2. Pour the coffee into a shallow dish. Dip each ladyfinger cookie into the coffee, being careful it does not fall apart. Arrange the cookies in a single layer in the bottom of a square baking dish.

3. Spread about one-third of the mascarpone cheese mixture over the cookies. Continue dipping the cookies into the coffee and create another layer on top of the mascarpone mixture. Once you have used up all the cookies, spread the remaining mascarpone mixture on top.

4. Cover and refrigerate for at least 1 hour. When you are ready to serve, generously sprinkle the cocoa powder over the top of the tiramisu.

PREP TIP: If you're hesitant about using raw eggs, you can cook the eggs in a double boiler over low heat, whisking constantly, for about 10 minutes or until they reach 160°F, or substitute pasteurized eggs.

Friendsgiving Feast

When we moved into our current apartment, beyond the large kitchen, the formal dining room was one of our favorite features. We could picture ourselves spending a lot of time in that room gathered around our big wooden table. In particular, we knew it would be the perfect place to host our annual Friendsgiving feast. Since college, a group of us have gathered every year for a big potluck celebration to give thanks and celebrate.

While it is true that a lot of work goes into hosting a big holiday, Thanksgiving is usually a meal that involves the whole group pitching in. We pull together a broad menu, and then everyone signs up to bring a dish. This menu is packed with our favorite recipes from Friendsgivings over the years. If you are hosting, plan to cook the bird, prep a few sides, and mix up a seasonal cocktail. Then, ask your guests to bring an appetizer or dessert.

We are also sharing our recipe for Leftover Turkey Potpie Hand Pies (page 179) so you can enjoy the plentiful leftovers that always accompany the Thanksgiving holiday.

Happy cooking, and happy Thanksgiving!

BURRATA & FIG CROSTINI	**169**
CRANBERRY & BRIE BITES	**170**
BRUSSELS SPROUTS GRATIN	**172**
CARAMELIZED SHALLOT & GARLIC MASHED POTATOES	**174**
LEMON-ROSEMARY ROASTED TURKEY	**175**
APPLE CINNAMON TARTLETS	**177**
CRANBERRY MULE	**178**
LEFTOVER TURKEY POTPIE HAND PIES	**179**

BURRATA & FIG CROSTINI

SERVES 6 | PREP TIME: 5 MINUTES | COOK TIME: 15 MINUTES

Cozy Comforts, Date Night, Meatless Monday, Nut Free, One Pot, Weeknight

Crostini in Italian means "little toast," and these little toasts are the perfect appetizer to kick off your Friendsgiving celebration. Each bite of crisp baguette topped with creamy burrata and sweet fig jam is a delight for the senses.

When prepping crostini in advance, we recommend toasting the baguette, then keeping the toppings separate until you are ready to serve so the crostini don't get soggy. Once guests arrive, assemble the toasts on a large wooden board or serving platter and watch them disappear.

½ **BAGUETTE, CUT INTO 12 PIECES**

2 **TABLESPOONS EXTRA-VIRGIN OLIVE OIL**

1 **CUP BURRATA CHEESE**

¼ **CUP FIG JAM**

2 **TABLESPOONS BALSAMIC VINEGAR**

1. Preheat the oven to 350°F. Line a baking sheet with parchment paper.

2. Drizzle the olive oil over the sliced baguette and place the pieces on the prepared baking sheet. Bake for 15 minutes, flipping the slices halfway through the baking time.

3. Spread 1 rounded tablespoon of burrata cheese on each piece of toasted bread. Top each with 1 teaspoon of fig jam. Drizzle with the vinegar and serve.

SWAP IT OUT: Burrata cheese is soft, spreadable, and perfect for crostini. If you don't love figs, feel free to use any jam you like, such as raspberry or strawberry. You can also skip the jam altogether in favor of sliced fresh fruit (we love fresh peaches!).

CRANBERRY & BRIE BITES

MAKES 24 BITES | PREP TIME: 55 MINUTES | COOK TIME: 20 MINUTES

Cozy Comforts, Date Night, Meatless Monday, Nut Free

When we do Thanksgiving with our families, there's always one certainty: someone will have purchased a can of cranberry sauce to satisfy Julien's single dinner request. There's something about that can-shaped blob that is nostalgic, and while it definitely isn't a delicacy, it's one thing that always screams Thanksgiving. We wanted to take that traditional holiday cranberry flavor and bring it to a small bite, so we pair it here with creamy Brie cheese for a delicious, yet simple, appetizer.

1 (8-OUNCE) PIECE BRIE CHEESE

NONSTICK COOKING SPRAY, FOR PREPARING THE MUFFIN PAN

1 PACKAGE PUFF PASTRY CUPS (24 PIECES)

½ CUP CRANBERRY SAUCE (CANNED OR HOMEMADE)

SEA SALT

1. Preheat the oven to 400°F.

2. Place the Brie cheese in the freezer for 20 minutes to firm up.

3. Meanwhile, coat a mini muffin pan with cooking spray. Place one puff pastry cup inside each muffin well and top with 1 teaspoon of cranberry sauce.

4. Remove the Brie from the freezer and cut it into 24 pieces. Push one piece of Brie into each of the pastry cups. Sprinkle lightly with salt. Refrigerate for 30 minutes.

5. Bake for 20 minutes.

> **KITCHEN HACK:** You can use regular muffin tins for this recipe if you don't have a mini muffin pan.

BRUSSELS SPROUTS GRATIN

SERVES 6 | PREP TIME: 10 MINUTES | COOK TIME: 1 HOUR

Cozy Comforts, Date Night, Nut Free

We're big Brussels sprouts fans. They seem to have gotten a bad rap while we were growing up, so we are always excited when we see them popping up at a restaurant or in a new recipe we try. They can be shaved in a salad or roasted in the oven—we'll eat them almost any way, except boiled beyond recognition! Here, we make them into a warm, bubbling gratin sure to lend a cozy vibe to your Friendsgiving Day.

8 OUNCES SLICED BACON, CHOPPED

1½ POUNDS BRUSSELS SPROUTS, TRIMMED AND QUARTERED

½ CUP (1 STICK) UNSALTED BUTTER, MELTED

1 SHALLOT, SLICED

4 GARLIC CLOVES, GRATED OR MINCED

3 THYME SPRIGS, LEAVES REMOVED AND CHOPPED

2 CUPS HEAVY (WHIPPING) CREAM

1 TABLESPOON DIJON MUSTARD

1 CUP GRATED PARMESAN CHEESE

¾ CUP SHREDDED GRUYÈRE CHEESE

1. Preheat the oven to 475°F.

2. Spread the bacon pieces in a single layer on a baking sheet and roast for 8 minutes, stirring once halfway through the cooking time.

3. In a large bowl, toss together the Brussels sprouts, melted butter, shallot, garlic, thyme, and cooked bacon until well combined.

4. Transfer to a 9-by-13-inch baking dish and roast on the bottom rack of the oven for 15 minutes. Carefully stir, then roast for 15 minutes more. Remove from the oven and reduce the oven temperature to 375°F.

5. In a small bowl, whisk together the heavy cream and mustard until fully combined.

6. Pour the cream mixture over the Brussels sprouts and top with the Parmesan and Gruyère cheeses, sprinkling them over the entire dish and covering evenly. Bake for 18 minutes or until the cream is bubbling.

7. Let cool for 10 minutes before serving.

KITCHEN HACK: Use ramekins to create individual portions to add a special touch to your Friendsgiving table. Cook for 10 to 15 minutes (depending on the number of ramekins in the oven) and check on them after 10 minutes.

CARAMELIZED SHALLOT & GARLIC MASHED POTATOES

SERVES 6 | PREP TIME: 10 MINUTES | COOK TIME: 30 MINUTES

Cozy Comforts, Date Night, Meatless Monday, Gluten Free, Nut Free

Classic mashed potatoes are a staple of any Thanksgiving meal, and there always seems to be leftovers for days. But this is Friendsgiving we're talking here, so let's shake things up a bit! By caramelizing the garlic and shallots, you build a lot of flavor that really packs a punch. If you do end up with leftovers, get them while you can, because someone may eat them before you get the chance!

2 POUNDS POTATOES, WASHED, PEELED, AND SLICED

8 GARLIC CLOVES, PEELED

9 TABLESPOONS UNSALTED BUTTER, CUT INTO TABLESPOON-SIZE PATS

4 SHALLOTS, THINLY SLICED

¼ CUP HEAVY (WHIPPING) CREAM

¼ CUP SOUR CREAM

2 TABLESPOONS MILK

SEA SALT

FRESHLY GROUND BLACK PEPPER

1. Bring a large pot of generously salted water to a boil over high heat. Carefully drop the sliced potatoes into the pot and cook for 20 minutes. Drain and set aside.

2. Using the flat edge of a large knife, smash the garlic cloves to flatten slightly.

3. In a cast-iron skillet over medium-low heat, melt 1 tablespoon of butter. Add the shallots and smashed garlic. Cook for 8 to 10, minutes until the shallots are softened and the garlic starts to brown.

4. Place the potatoes in a large bowl with the remaining 8 tablespoons of butter. Using a hand masher, mash the potatoes with the butter. Once the butter has melted, add the heavy cream, sour cream, and milk and continue to mash until your potatoes are smooth.

5. Using a rubber spatula, fold in the garlic and shallots, stirring well to combine. Season with salt and pepper.

LEMON-ROSEMARY ROASTED TURKEY

SERVES 6 | PREP TIME: 40 MINUTES | COOK TIME: 2 HOURS, 30 MINUTES |
REST TIME: 30 MINUTES

Cozy Comforts, Date Night, Meatless Monday, Gluten Free, Dairy Free, Nut Free, One Pot

Here it is: the Big Bird. We have made this turkey recipe countless times for Thanksgivings, Easters, Friendsgivings—you name it! We were both intimidated the first time we were responsible for making this main course, but with some patience (and a ton of research—you should have seen the history on our web browsers) we ended up with a super moist turkey we've been recreating ever since. The key is baking it low and slow, and making sure you time the baking of your other dishes so you aren't constantly opening and closing the oven. Enjoy!

1 (12-POUND)
TURKEY, THAWED

2 TABLESPOONS OLIVE OIL

6 TABLESPOONS UNSALTED
BUTTER, CUT INTO
TABLESPOON-SIZE PATS

8 ROSEMARY SPRIGS

2 LEMONS, SLICED

1 WHITE ONION, HALVED

SEA SALT

FRESHLY GROUND
BLACK PEPPER

1 CUP VEGETABLE STOCK

1. Remove the turkey from the refrigerator at least 30 minutes before you plan to roast it. Check the cavity for the giblets and neck and remove these, if needed. Place the turkey, breast-side up, in a roasting pan.

2. Preheat the oven to 450°F, with just one rack in the oven in the bottom position.

3. Drizzle the olive oil over the entire turkey and use your hands to rub the oil into the turkey's skin.

4. Using a small, sharp knife, make six incisions in the top of the turkey. Use your finger to carefully loosen the skin around the incisions and insert one pat of butter into each incision.

5. Using your hands, break two rosemary sprigs into smaller pieces. Slide these into the incisions alongside the butter.

6. Place the remaining six rosemary sprigs, the lemon slices, and onion halves inside the turkey cavity.

(Continued)

7. Sprinkle salt and pepper over the entire turkey. Use kitchen twine to tie the legs together. Alternately, truss the entire turkey.

8. Pour the vegetable stock into the roasting pan.

9. Turn the oven temperature to 350°F and place the turkey in the oven. Roast for about 2½ hours or until several areas of the turkey reach an internal temperature of 165°F on an instant-read thermometer. If the turkey's breast meat starts to brown more quickly than it reaches temperature, place a piece of aluminum foil over the top to prevent it from overcooking.

10. Remove the turkey from the oven and transfer it to a large, clean cutting board. Cover the top of the turkey with foil and let rest for 25 to 30 minutes before carving.

SWAP IT OUT: We love the light, bright flavors lemon and rosemary provide while roasting inside the turkey's cavity. You can swap these out to include a variety of vegetables, such as carrots or parsnips—or even homemade stuffing. If you decide to stuff the turkey's cavity, pay extra attention to the roasting time, as this will increase the time needed to reach the appropriate temperature of 165°F.

APPLE CINNAMON TARTLETS

SERVES 6 | PREP TIME: 5 MINUTES | COOK TIME: 12 MINUTES

Cozy Comforts, Date Night, Meatless Monday, Nut Free, One Pot, Weeknight

One of our favorite things about these tartlets is how easy they are to put together—a key element of a successful Friendsgiving menu. By using the crescent roll dough (a quick grocery store shortcut), you can whip these up in no time so you get to spend more time with your guests. And the best part? Everyone gets their own!

2 PACKAGES REFRIGERATED CRESCENT ROLL DOUGH

1½ TABLESPOONS SUGAR, DIVIDED

1½ TABLESPOONS GROUND CINNAMON, DIVIDED

2 APPLES, CORED AND THINLY SLICED (WE LIKE GRANNY SMITHS FOR THIS)

1. Preheat the oven to 375°F.

2. Open the crescent roll dough on a baking sheet and create six rectangles, using your fingers to seal the perforations that appear on the dough. Sprinkle with half the sugar and half the cinnamon, and bake for 5 minutes.

3. Remove the tartlets from the oven and top each with apple slices. Sprinkle with the remaining sugar and cinnamon and bake for 7 minutes more.

> **MIX IT UP:** These tartlets are the perfect vessel for some ice cream! Top with a scoop of your favorite flavor (we're apple pie traditionalists, so we choose vanilla) and serve immediately.

CRANBERRY MULE

SERVES 6 | PREP TIME: 5 MINUTES

Cozy Comforts, Dairy Free, Date Night, Gluten Free, Meatless Monday, Nut Free, One Pot, Weeknight

Here in Massachusetts, we are lucky to have tons of local cranberry bogs. The fresh fruit is generally picked right at the start of autumn, so as an ode to the fall harvest of our state berry, we put a Friendsgiving spin on the classic Moscow Mule. The sweetness of the cranberry juice is the perfect complement to the warm, spicy taste of ginger beer.

24 OUNCES (2 CANS) GINGER BEER

12 OUNCES VODKA

1½ CUPS CRANBERRY JUICE

JUICE OF 6 LIMES

ICE CUBES

In a large pitcher, combine the ginger beer, vodka, cranberry juice, lime juice, and ice cubes. Stir well and serve in mule cups (or any cup you choose).

LEFTOVER TURKEY POTPIE HAND PIES

SERVES 6 | PREP TIME: 20 MINUTES | COOK TIME: 25 MINUTES

Cozy Comforts, Nut Free

Leftovers are great for lunch the day after your dinner party. Instead of the regular reheat, why not repurpose them into a totally new meal? This recipe will help you use up any leftover Lemon-Rosemary Roasted Turkey (page 175) you might have by pairing it with veggies and turning it into a creamy, flavorful filling for a crispy-crusted hand pie. Assembly of the pies is required, so grab your partner and make this into a group activity!

3 TABLESPOONS UNSALTED BUTTER

1 SMALL ONION, DICED

1 CARROT, DICED

1 CELERY STALK, DICED

¼ CUP ALL-PURPOSE FLOUR

¾ CUP VEGETABLE STOCK

¾ CUP MILK

¼ CUP HEAVY (WHIPPING) CREAM

4 TABLESPOONS CREAM CHEESE, AT ROOM TEMPERATURE

2 CUPS SHREDDED LEFTOVER LEMON-ROSEMARY ROASTED TURKEY (PAGE 175)

½ CUP PEAS

1 TEASPOON SALT

½ TEASPOON GARLIC POWDER

½ TEASPOON DRIED ROSEMARY

½ TEASPOON FRESHLY GROUND BLACK PEPPER

1 PACKAGE REFRIGERATED PIECRUSTS

1 EGG

1 TABLESPOON WATER

(Continued page 180)

1. Preheat the oven to 400°F. Line a baking sheet with parchment paper and set aside.

2. In a large skillet over medium heat, melt the butter. Add the onion, carrot, and celery and cook for 5 minutes.

3. Sprinkle the flour over the vegetables and stir to coat. Cook for 1 minute.

4. While stirring, slowly add the vegetable stock, milk, and heavy cream.

5. Add the cream cheese, breaking it apart with the edge of a spoon or spatula so it can melt into the sauce. Cook for 1 to 2 minutes, until the sauce is thickened.

6. Add the leftover turkey, peas, salt, garlic powder, rosemary, and pepper and stir. Remove from the heat and set aside.

7. Unfold the piecrusts and use a rolling pin to make them slightly thinner. Using a 6-inch-diameter bowl as a guide, cut 6 circles from the piecrusts. You may need to use the rolling pin to combine and re-roll the scraps to have enough crust.

8. Spoon the turkey mixture onto one half of each circle, fitting as much as you can while leaving a slight edge visible on the filled side.

9. In a small bowl, whisk the egg and water. Dip a pastry brush (or your fingers) into the egg wash and moisten the edge all the way around each circle. Fold the empty half of each dough circle over the top of the turkey mixture to create a half-moon, pressing to seal the edges together. Use a fork to crimp the edges.

10. Place the hand pies on the prepared baking sheet and brush the tops of each pie with the remaining egg wash. Bake for 15 minutes or until golden.

KITCHEN HACK: You can make the filling (steps 2 through 6) a day in advance if you like. Once the filling has cooked, refrigerate it in a covered bowl or container.

Sauces & Extras

CHOCOLATE-HAZELNUT SPREAD **183**

TZATZIKI **184**

5-INGREDIENT PESTO **185**

CHOCOLATE-HAZELNUT SPREAD

MAKES 1 CUP | PREP TIME: 15 MINUTES | COOK TIME: 15 MINUTES

Cozy Comforts, Dairy Free, Date Night, Gluten Free, Weeknight

1¼ CUPS HAZELNUTS

1 CUP DARK CHOCOLATE CHIPS

1. Preheat the oven to 350°F.

2. Arrange the hazelnuts on a rimmed baking sheet; bake for about 10 minutes or until golden brown. Remove from the oven and let cool for 5 minutes, then carefully remove the skins from the hazelnuts by rubbing them in a clean kitchen towel.

3. Meanwhile, assemble a double boiler over medium heat. Put the chocolate in the bowl on top, and stir until it is completely melted.

4. Transfer the hazelnuts to a food processor and grind for about 30 seconds or until it is creamy.

5. Pour the melted chocolate into the food processor and pulse until it is completely combined and smooth.

> **MAKE-AHEAD TIP:** Make this recipe in advance, and refrigerate it in an airtight container for up to two weeks.

TZATZIKI

MAKES 2½ CUPS | PREP TIME: 10 MINUTES, PLUS 1 HOUR TO CHILL

Cozy Comforts, Gluten Free, Date Night, Meatless Monday, Nut Free, Weeknight

1 ENGLISH (SEEDLESS) CUCUMBER, PEELED

SEA SALT

2 CUPS PLAIN GREEK YOGURT

3 GARLIC CLOVES, MINCED

JUICE OF ½ LEMON

2 TABLESPOONS CHOPPED FRESH DILL

FRESHLY GROUND BLACK PEPPER

1. Line a small bowl with paper towels.

2. Use a box or handheld grater to grate the cucumber into the prepared bowl. Sprinkle salt over top and stir to mix it in. Let the cucumber sit for 15 minutes to draw out the water. Squeeze out as much liquid as possible, and set the cucumber aside.

3. In a medium bowl, stir together the yogurt, garlic, lemon juice, and dill. Add the grated cucumber and stir to combine. Season with salt and pepper. Refrigerate for at least 1 hour before serving or using.

5-INGREDIENT PESTO

MAKES 2 CUPS | PREP TIME: 15 MINUTES

Cozy Comforts, Date Night, Gluten Free, Meatless Monday, One Pot, Weeknight

6 CUPS PACKED FRESH BASIL

1 CUP PINE NUTS

6 GARLIC CLOVES, COARSELY CHOPPED

SEA SALT

1 CUP EXTRA-VIRGIN OLIVE OIL

⅔ CUP FINELY GRATED PARMESAN CHEESE

In a food processor, combine the basil, pine nuts, and garlic and season with salt. Turn the processor on and slowly stream in the olive oil until the ingredients are fully combined. Add the Parmesan cheese and pulse to combine.

MAKE-AHEAD TIP: Make this recipe in advance, and refrigerate it in an airtight container for four to five days.

MEASUREMENT CONVERSIONS

VOLUME EQUIVALENTS (LIQUID)

US STANDARD	US STANDARD (OUNCES)	METRIC (APPROXIMATE)
2 tablespoons	1 fl. oz.	30 ml
¼ cup	2 fl. oz.	60 ml
½ cup	4 fl. oz.	120 ml
1 cup	8 fl. oz.	240 ml
1½ cups	12 fl. oz.	355 ml
2 cups or 1 pint	16 fl. oz.	475 ml
4 cups or 1 quart	32 fl. oz.	1 L
1 gallon	128 fl. oz.	4 L

OVEN TEMPERATURES

FAHRENHEIT	CELSIUS (APPROXIMATE)
250°F	120°C
300°F	150°C
325°F	165°C
350°F	180°C
375°F	190°C
400°F	200°C
425°F	220°C
450°F	230°C

VOLUME EQUIVALENTS (DRY)

US STANDARD	METRIC (APPROXIMATE)
⅛ teaspoon	0.5 mL
¼ teaspoon	1 mL
½ teaspoon	2 mL
¾ teaspoon	4 mL
1 teaspoon	5 mL
1 tablespoon	15 mL
¼ cup	59 mL
⅓ cup	79 mL
½ cup	118 mL
⅔ cup	156 mL
¾ cup	177 mL
1 cup	235 mL
2 cups or 1 pint	475 mL
3 cups	700 mL
4 cups or 1 quart	1 L

WEIGHT EQUIVALENTS

US STANDARD	METRIC (APPROXIMATE)
½ ounce	15 g
1 ounce	30 g
2 ounces	60 g
4 ounces	115 g
8 ounces	225 g
12 ounces	340 g
16 ounces or 1 pound	455 g

THE DIRTY DOZEN
& THE CLEAN FIFTEEN™

The **DIRTY DOZEN** are foods that have high levels of pesticide residues when conventionally grown. In 2014, the Environmental Working Group recommended buying the organic versions of the following whenever possible:

» Apples
» Celery
» Cherry tomatoes
» Cucumbers
» Grapes
» Nectarines
» Peaches
» Potatoes
» Snap peas
» Spinach
» Strawberries
» Sweet bell peppers

The **CLEAN FIFTEEN** were found to have the lowest amounts of pesticide contamination in 2014, and are considered safe to buy conventionally grown (nonorganic):

» Asparagus
» Avocados
» Cabbage
» Cantaloupe (domestic)
» Cauliflower
» Eggplants
» Grapefruits
» Kiwis
» Mangos
» Onions
» Papayas
» Pineapples
» Sweet corn
» Sweet peas (frozen)
» Sweet potatoes

INDEX

A

Adult Lemonade, 155

Aperol Spritz, 160

Apple Cinnamon Tartlets, 177

Artichoke hearts
    Spinach Artichoke Dip, 58–59

Arugula
    Prosciutto & Pear Arugula
        Salad, 41

Asparagus
    Cod & Vegetables en
        Papillote, 98
    Parmesan Roasted
        Asparagus, 50

Avocados
    Mini Avocado & Ricotta
        Toasts, 135

B

Bacon. *See also* Pancetta
    Bacon-Wrapped Dates, 123
    Breakfast Sandwiches on
        Toasted Brioche, 28–29
    Brussels Sprouts
        Gratin, 172–173
    Easy Bacon & Broccoli
        Strata, 138
    Eggs & Bacon Fried
        Rice, 26–27
    Tomato & Bacon Grilled
        Cheese, 66

Baked Lobster Macaroni &
    Cheese, 102–103

Bakeware, 5

Barware, 5

Basil
    Caprese Salad Skewers, 157
    Creamy Tomato Soup, 56

Garlic & Herb Filet
    Mignon, 84
Strawberry-Basil Sorbet, 105
Tomato Tart with
    Burrata, 61

BBQ, Weekend, 146–155

Beans. *See also* Green beans
    Southwest Chicken &
        Avocado Salad, 46–47
    White Bean Hummus, 57

Beef
    Beef Wellington
        Bites, 126–127
    Classic Beef Stew, 78–79
    Garlic & Herb Filet
        Mignon, 84
    Homemade Burger
        Bar, 150–151

Berries
    Chocolate Hazelnut Crepes
        with Fresh
        Strawberries, 30–31
    Homemade Granola &
        Yogurt Parfait, 20
    Mimosa Bar, 139
    Mixed Berry Dutch Baby, 32
    Peach & Raspberry
        Cobbler, 112–113
    Prosecco Ice Pops, 132
    Simple Fruit Salad, 136
    Strawberry-Basil Sorbet, 105
    Strawberry
        Shortcake, 110–111

Beverages
    Adult Lemonade, 155
    Aperol Spritz, 160
    Bourbon & Peach Tea
        Punch, 131

Cranberry Mule, 178
Mimosa Bar, 139
Paloma Cocktails, 130
Pumpkin Spice Iced
    Coffee, 144

Birthday Brunch, 134–144

Blenders, 3

Blue cheese
    Blue Cheese–Stuffed
        Olives, 122
    Buffalo Chicken
        Meatballs, 64

Boards
    Italian Cheese &
        Charcuterie Board, 158
    Perfect Grazing Board,
        The, 128–129

Bourbon & Peach Tea
    Punch, 131

Bread Pudding for Two, 107

Breakfast Sandwiches on
    Toasted Brioche, 28–29

Brie
    Cranberry & Brie Bites, 170

Broccoli
    Easy Bacon & Broccoli
        Strata, 138
    Roasted Asian-Style
        Broccoli, 48

Broccoli Rabe, Garlic
    Sautéed, 162

Brunch, Birthday, 134–144

Brussels Sprouts
    Gratin, 172–173

Buffalo Chicken
    Meatballs, 64

Bulk-shopping, 10

Burrata & Fig Crostini, 169

Burrata cheese
  Burrata & Fig Crostini, 169
  Tomato Tart with
    Burrata, 61

C

Cabbage
  Simple Asian Salad with
    Ginger Dressing, 45
Cacio e Pepe, 91–92
Caprese Salad Skewers, 157
Caramelized Onion Dip, 147
Caramelized Shallot & Garlic
  Mashed Potatoes, 174
Carbonara Risotto, 80–81
Carnitas Tacos with Pickled
  Red Onion & Slaw, 76–77
Carrots
  Buffalo Chicken
    Meatballs, 64
  Classic Beef Stew, 78–79
  Cod & Vegetables en
    Papillote, 98
  Leftover Turkey Potpie
    Hand Pies, 179–181
  Simple Asian Salad with
    Ginger Dressing, 45
Cauliflower & Ricotta
  Pizza, 89–90
Cheddar cheese
  Baked Lobster Macaroni &
    Cheese, 102–103
  Breakfast Sandwiches on
    Toasted Brioche, 28–29
  Easy Bacon & Broccoli
    Strata, 138
Cheese. See specific
Cheesecakes, Mini, 114–115
Chicken
  Buffalo Chicken Meatballs, 64
  Chicken & Chickpea Tikka
    Masala, 70–71

Chicken
  Saltimbocca, 164–165
  Creamy Sun-Dried
    Tomato Chicken
    Pasta, 74–75
  Easy Chicken & Shiitake
    Ramen, 69
  Gochujang BBQ
    Chicken, 152
  Grilled Chicken & Romaine
    Caesar, 42–43
  Prosciutto-Wrapped
    Chicken, 68
  Southwest Chicken &
    Avocado Salad, 46–47
  Spicy Chicken Bites, 65
  Thai Red Curry
    Chicken, 72–73
Chickpeas
  Chicken & Chickpea Tikka
    Masala, 70–71
  Chopped Kale Greek
    Salad, 44
  Falafel Gyros with
    Tzatziki, 85–86
Chili Roasted Sweet
  Potatoes, 52
Chives
  Easy Bacon and Broccoli
    Strata, 138
Chocolate
  Chocolate Cake with
    Buttercream
    Frosting, 142–143
  Chocolate Chip Skillet
    Cookie, 119
  Chocolate-Hazelnut
    Spread, 183
  Chocolate Mousse, 106
  Mug Brownies à la
    Mode, 116
  Stracciatella
    Semifreddo, 118

Chocolate-Hazelnut
  Spread, 183
  Chocolate Hazelnut Crepes
    with Fresh
    Strawberries, 30–31
  Stracciatella
    Semifreddo, 118
Chopped Kale Greek Salad, 44
Cilantro
  Chicken & Chickpea Tikka
    Masala, 70–71
  Elote Corn Salad, 149
  Shrimp Pad Thai, 100–101
  Southwest Chicken &
    Avocado Salad, 46–47
  Thai Red Curry
    Chicken, 72–73
Cinnamon Rolls, Giant, 37–39
Classic Beef Stew, 78–79
Cocktail parties, 12, 121–131
Coconut milk
  Chicken & Chickpea Tikka
    Masala, 70–71
  Coconut Sticky Rice, 53–54
  Thai Red Curry
    Chicken, 72–73
Coconut Sticky Rice, 53–54
Cod and Vegetables en
  Papillote, 98
Coffee
  Coffee Crème
    Brûlée, 108–109
  Pumpkin Spice Iced
    Coffee, 144
  Simple Tiramisu, 166
Coffee Cake Muffins, 137
Corn
  Elote Corn Salad, 149
  Southwest Chicken &
    Avocado Salad, 46–47
  Summer Veggie Orecchiette
    and Pesto, 87–88

Corn Bread Muffins, 55

Cornmeal
Corn Bread Muffins, 55
Peach & Raspberry
Cobbler, 112–113

Cotija cheese
Elote Corn Salad, 149

Cozy Comforts
Adult Lemonade, 155
Aperol Spritz, 160
Apple Cinnamon
Tartlets, 177
Baked Lobster Macaroni &
Cheese, 102–103
Beef Wellington
Bites, 126–127
Bread Pudding for Two, 107
Breakfast Sandwiches on
Toasted Brioche, 28–29
Brussels Sprouts
Gratin, 172–173
Burrata & Fig Crostini, 169
Cacio e Pepe, 91–92
Caprese Salad Skewers, 157
Caramelized Onion Dip, 147
Caramelized Shallot &
Garlic Mashed
Potatoes, 174
Carbonara Risotto, 80–81
Carnitas Tacos with Pickled
Red Onion & Slaw, 76–77
Cauliflower & Ricotta
Pizza, 89–90
Chicken
Saltimbocca, 164–165
Chocolate Chip Skillet
Cookie, 119
Chocolate Hazelnut Crepes
with Fresh
Strawberries, 30–31
Chocolate-Hazelnut
Spread, 183
Classic Beef Stew, 78–79

Coconut Sticky
Rice, 53–54
Coffee Crème
Brûlée, 108–109
Corn Bread Muffins, 55
Cranberry & Brie Bites, 170
Cranberry Mule, 178
Creamy Sun-Dried Tomato
Chicken Pasta, 74–75
Creamy Tomato & Sausage
Rigatoni, 82–83
Creamy Tomato Soup, 56
Deviled Eggs, 146
Easy Bacon & Broccoli
Strata, 138
Easy Chicken & Shiitake
Ramen, 69
Eggs & Bacon Fried
Rice, 26–27
Eggs Benedict
Florentine, 21–22
Elote Corn Salad, 149
5-Ingredient Pesto, 185
French Toast with Peaches
and Honey, 35–36
Garlic & Herb Filet
Mignon, 84
Garlic Sautéed Broccoli
Rabe, 162
Giant Cinnamon
Rolls, 37–39
Gochujang BBQ
Chicken, 152
Grilled Zucchini with
Lemon Zest, 161
Homemade Burger
Bar, 150–151
Homemade Crispy
Waffles, 33–34
Homemade Pizza
Rolls, 62–63
Italian Cheese &
Charcuterie Board, 158

Leftover Turkey Potpie
Hand Pies, 179–181
Lemon-Rosemary Roasted
Turkey, 175–176
Loaf Pan Eggplant
Lasagna, 93–94
Mini Cheesecakes, 114–115
Mixed Berry Dutch
Baby, 32
Mug Brownies à la
Mode, 116
Mussels in White Wine &
Garlic with Crusty
Bread, 96–97
Peach & Raspberry
Cobbler, 112–113
Peanut Butter Cup
S'mores, 154
Prosciutto-Wrapped
Chicken, 68
Pumpkin Spice Iced
Coffee, 144
Shrimp Pad Thai, 100–101
Simple Tiramisu, 166
Spicy Chicken Bites, 65
Spinach Artichoke
Dip, 58–59
Sprinkle-Loaded
Waffles, 141
Stracciatella
Semifreddo, 118
Strawberry
Shortcake, 110–111
Thai Red Curry
Chicken, 72–73
Tomato & Bacon Grilled
Cheese, 66
Tomato Tart with
Burrata, 61
Trofie al Pesto, 163
Tzatziki, 184
Cranberry & Brie Bites, 170
Cranberry Mule, 178

Cream cheese
  Caramelized Onion Dip, 147
  Giant Cinnamon
    Rolls, 37–39
  Leftover Turkey Potpie
    Hand Pies, 179–181
  Mini Cheesecakes, 114–115
  Spinach Artichoke
    Dip, 58–59
  Stracciatella Semifreddo, 118
Creamy Sun-Dried Tomato
  Chicken Pasta, 74–75
Creamy Tomato & Sausage
  Rigatoni, 82–83
Creamy Tomato Soup, 56
Crispy Garlic Green Beans, 49
Cucumbers
  Chopped Kale Greek
    Salad, 44
  Falafel Gyros with
    Tzatziki, 85–86
  Tzatziki, 184
Cutting boards, 6

D
Dairy Free
  Adult Lemonade, 155
  Aperol Spritz, 160
  Apple Cinnamon
    Tartlets, 177
  Bacon-Wrapped Dates, 123
  Beef Wellington
    Bites, 126–127
  Bourbon & Peach Tea
    Punch, 131
  Carnitas Tacos with
    Pickled Red Onion &
    Slaw, 76–77
  Chili Roasted Sweet
    Potatoes, 52
  Chocolate-Hazelnut
    Spread, 183

Classic Beef Stew, 78–79
Coconut Sticky Rice, 53–54
Cod and Vegetables en
  Papillote, 98
Cranberry Mule, 178
Crispy Garlic Green
  Beans, 49
Deviled Eggs, 146
Eggs & Bacon Fried
  Rice, 26–27
Eggs Benedict
  Florentine, 21–22
Garlic & Herb Filet
  Mignon, 84
Garlic Sautéed Broccoli
  Rabe, 162
Gochujang BBQ
  Chicken, 152
Grilled Zucchini with
  Lemon Zest, 161
Honey Sriracha-Glazed
  Salmon, 95
Lemon-Rosemary Roasted
  Turkey, 175–176
Mimosa Bar, 139
Paloma Cocktails, 130
Prosciutto-Wrapped
  Chicken, 68
Prosecco Ice Pops, 132
Roasted Asian-Style
  Broccoli, 48
Roasted Rosemary
  Potatoes, 51
Shrimp Pad Thai, 100–101
Simple Asian Salad with
  Ginger Dressing, 45
Simple Fruit Salad, 136
Spicy Chicken Bites, 65
Strawberry-Basil
  Sorbet, 105
Thai Red Curry
  Chicken, 72–73
White Bean Hummus, 57

Date Night
  Adult Lemonade, 155
  Aperol Spritz, 160
  Apple Cinnamon
    Tartlets, 177
  Baked Lobster Macaroni &
    Cheese, 102–103
  Bread Pudding for Two, 107
  Brussels Sprouts
    Gratin, 172–173
  Burrata & Fig Crostini, 169
  Caprese Salad Skewers, 157
  Caramelized Shallot &
    Garlic Mashed
    Potatoes, 174
  Carbonara Risotto, 80–81
  Carnitas Tacos with Pickled
    Red Onion & Slaw, 76–77
  Chicken
    Saltimbocca, 164–165
  Chili Roasted Sweet
    Potatoes, 52
  Chocolate Chip Skillet
    Cookie, 119
  Chocolate-Hazelnut
    Spread, 183
  Chocolate Mousse, 106
  Classic Beef Stew, 78–79
  Coconut Sticky Rice, 53–54
  Coffee Crème
    Brûlée, 108–109
  Corn Bread Muffins, 55
  Cranberry & Brie Bites, 170
  Cranberry Mule, 178
  Crispy Garlic Green Beans, 49
  Deviled Eggs, 146
  Elote Corn Salad, 149
  5-Ingredient Pesto, 185
  Garlic Sautéed Broccoli
    Rabe, 162
  Gochujang BBQ
    Chicken, 152

Date Night (*Continued*)

    Grilled Zucchini with
        Lemon Zest, 161

    Homemade Burger
        Bar, 150–151

    Honey Sriracha-Glazed
        Salmon, 95

    Italian Cheese &
        Charcuterie Board, 158

    Lemon-Rosemary Roasted
        Turkey, 175–176

    Loaf Pan Eggplant
        Lasagna, 93–94

    Mini Cheesecakes, 114–115

    Mussels in White Wine &
        Garlic with Crusty
        Bread, 96–97

    Parmesan Roasted
        Asparagus, 50

    Peach & Raspberry
        Cobbler, 112–113

    Pumpkin Spice Iced
        Coffee, 144

    Roasted Asian-Style
        Broccoli, 48

    Roasted Rosemary
        Potatoes, 51

    Simple Tiramisu, 166

    Sprinkle-Loaded
        Waffles, 141

    Stracciatella Semifreddo, 118

    Strawberry-Basil Sorbet, 105

    Tzatziki, 184

    Watermelon & Feta
        Salad, 148

Dates, Bacon-Wrapped, 123

Desserts

    Apple Cinnamon
        Tartlets, 177

    Bread Pudding for Two, 107

    Chocolate Chip Skillet
        Cookie, 119

    Chocolate Mousse, 106

    Coffee Crème
        Brûlée, 108–109

    Mini Cheesecakes, 114–115

    Mug Brownies à la
        Mode, 116

    Peach & Raspberry
        Cobbler, 112–113

    Peanut Butter Cup
        S'mores, 154

    Simple Tiramisu, 166

    Stracciatella Semifreddo, 118

    Strawberry-Basil
        Sorbet, 105

    Strawberry
        Shortcake, 110–111

Deviled Eggs, 146

Dill

    Tzatziki, 184

Dinner parties, 13, 156–166

Dishware, 5

Dutch ovens, 3

E

Easy Bacon & Broccoli
    Strata, 138

Easy Chicken & Shiitake
    Ramen, 69

Edamame

    Simple Asian Salad with
        Ginger Dressing, 45

Eggplant Lasagna, Loaf
    Pan, 93–94

Eggs

    Breakfast Sandwiches on
        Toasted Brioche, 28–29

    Coffee Crème
        Brûlée, 108–109

    Deviled Eggs, 146

    Easy Bacon & Broccoli
        Strata, 138

    Eggs & Bacon Fried
        Rice, 26–27

Eggs Benedict
    Florentine, 21–22

Simple Tiramisu, 166

Tomato, Spinach & Goat
    Cheese Omelets, 24–25

Elote Corn Salad, 149

Equipment, 2–6

F

Falafel Gyros with
    Tzatziki, 85–86

Feta cheese

    Chopped Kale Greek
        Salad, 44

    Falafel Gyros with
        Tzatziki, 85–86

    Watermelon & Feta
        Salad, 148

Fig jam

    Burrata & Fig Crostini, 169

Fish

    Cod & Vegetables en
        Papillote, 98

    Honey Sriracha-Glazed
        Salmon, 95

5-Ingredient Pesto, 185

Flatware, 5

Food processors, 3

French Toast with
    Peaches and
    Honey, 35–36

Friendsgiving feast, 168–181

G

Garlic & Herb Filet
    Mignon, 84

Garlic Sautéed Broccoli
    Rabe, 162

Giant Cinnamon Rolls, 37–39

Ginger

    Crispy Garlic Green
        Beans, 49

Easy Chicken & Shiitake Ramen, 69

Simple Asian Salad with Ginger Dressing, 45

Gluten Free

Adult Lemonade, 155

Aperol Spritz, 160

Bacon-Wrapped Dates, 123

Blue Cheese-Stuffed Olives, 122

Bourbon & Peach Tea Punch, 131

Caprese Salad Skewers, 157

Caramelized Shallot & Garlic Mashed Potatoes, 174

Carbonara Risotto, 80–81

Carnitas Tacos with Pickled Red Onion & Slaw, 76–77

Chicken Saltimbocca, 164–165

Chili Roasted Sweet Potatoes, 52

Chocolate-Hazelnut Spread, 183

Chocolate Mousse, 106

Chopped Kale Greek Salad, 44

Coconut Sticky Rice, 53–54

Cod & Vegetables en Papillote, 98

Coffee Crème Brûlée, 108–109

Cranberry Mule, 178

Creamy Tomato Soup, 56

Deviled Eggs, 146

Elote Corn Salad, 149

5-Ingredient Pesto, 185

Garlic & Herb Filet Mignon, 84

Garlic Sautéed Broccoli Rabe, 162

Grilled Chicken & Romaine Caesar, 42–43

Grilled Zucchini with Lemon Zest, 161

Lemon-Rosemary Roasted Turkey, 175–176

Loaf Pan Eggplant Lasagna, 93–94

Mimosa Bar, 139

Paloma Cocktails, 130

Potato & Chorizo Bites, 124–125

Prosciutto & Pear Arugula Salad, 41

Prosciutto-Wrapped Chicken, 68

Prosecco Ice Pops, 132

Pumpkin Spice Iced Coffee, 144

Roasted Rosemary Potatoes, 51

Shrimp Pad Thai, 100–101

Simple Fruit Salad, 136

Southwest Chicken & Avocado Salad, 46–47

Spinach Artichoke Dip, 58–59

Stracciatella Semifreddo, 118

Strawberry-Basil Sorbet, 105

Thai Red Curry Chicken, 72–73

Tomato, Spinach & Goat Cheese Omelets, 24–25

Tzatziki, 184

Watermelon & Feta Salad, 148

White Bean Hummus, 57

Goat cheese

Prosciutto & Pear Arugula Salad, 41

Tomato, Spinach & Goat Cheese Omelets, 24–25

Gochujang BBQ Chicken, 152

Grapes

Simple Fruit Salad, 136

Green Beans, Crispy Garlic, 49

Grilled Chicken & Romaine Caesar, 42–43

Grilled Zucchini with Lemon Zest, 161

Gruyère cheese

Baked Lobster Macaroni & Cheese, 102–103

Brussels Sprouts Gratin, 172–173

Tomato & Bacon Grilled Cheese, 66

H

Homemade Burger Bar, 150–151

Homemade Crispy Waffles, 33–34

Homemade Granola & Yogurt Parfait, 20

Homemade Pizza Rolls, 62–63

Honey Sriracha-Glazed Salmon, 95

Hosting, 12–13

Hummus, White Bean, 57

I

Ingredients, 8–9

Italian Cheese & Charcuterie Board, 158

K

Kale Greek Salad, Chopped, 44

"Kitchen triangle," 7–8

Kiwi fruits

Simple Fruit Salad, 136

Knives, 3, 6

L

Leftovers, 11–13

Leftover Turkey Potpie Hand Pies, 179–181

Lemon-Rosemary Roasted
Turkey, 175–176
Lettuce
Grilled Chicken & Romaine
Caesar, 42–43
Simple Asian Salad with
Ginger Dressing, 45
Southwest Chicken &
Avocado Salad, 46–47
Loaf Pan Eggplant
Lasagna, 93–94
Lobster Macaroni & Cheese,
Baked, 102–103

M

Mangoes
Prosecco Ice Pops, 132
Simple Fruit Salad, 136
Mascarpone cheese
Simple Tiramisu, 166
Meatballs, Buffalo
Chicken, 64
Meatless Monday
Adult Lemonade, 155
Aperol Spritz, 160
Apple Cinnamon
Tartlets, 177
Bread Pudding for Two, 107
Burrata & Fig Crostini, 169
Cacio e Pepe, 91–92
Caprese Salad Skewers, 157
Caramelized Onion Dip, 147
Caramelized Shallot &
Garlic Mashed
Potatoes, 174
Cauliflower & Ricotta
Pizza, 89–90
Chili Roasted Sweet
Potatoes, 52
Chocolate Chip Skillet
Cookie, 119
Chopped Kale Greek
Salad, 44

Cod & Vegetables en
Papillote, 98
Coffee Crème
Brûlée, 108–109
Corn Bread Muffins, 55
Cranberry & Brie Bites, 170
Cranberry Mule, 178
Creamy Tomato Soup, 56
Crispy Garlic Green
Beans, 49
Deviled Eggs, 146
Elote Corn Salad, 149
Falafel Gyros with
Tzatziki, 85–86
5-Ingredient Pesto, 185
French Toast with Peaches
and Honey, 35–36
Garlic Sautéed Broccoli
Rabe, 162
Giant Cinnamon
Rolls, 37–39
Grilled Zucchini with
Lemon Zest, 161
Homemade Crispy
Waffles, 33–34
Homemade Granola &
Yogurt Parfait, 20
Lemon-Rosemary Roasted
Turkey, 175–176
Loaf Pan Eggplant
Lasagna, 93–94
Mini Cheesecakes, 114–115
Mixed Berry Dutch Baby, 32
Mug Brownies à la
Mode, 116
Mussels in White Wine &
Garlic with Crusty
Bread, 96–97
Parmesan Roasted
Asparagus, 50
Peanut Butter Cup
S'mores, 154
Pumpkin Spice Iced
Coffee, 144

Roasted Asian-Style
Broccoli, 48
Roasted Rosemary
Potatoes, 51
Simple Asian Salad with
Ginger Dressing, 45
Simple Tiramisu, 166
Sprinkle-Loaded Waffles, 141
Stracciatella Semifreddo, 118
Strawberry
Shortcake, 110–111
Summer Veggie Orecchiette
& Pesto, 87–88
Tomato, Spinach & Goat
Cheese Omelets, 24–25
Tomato Tart with Burrata, 61
Trofie al Pesto, 163
Tzatziki, 184
Watermelon & Feta
Salad, 148
Mimosa Bar, 139
Mini Avocado & Ricotta
Toasts, 135
Mini Cheesecakes, 114–115
Mint
Watermelon & Feta
Salad, 148
Mixed Berry Dutch Baby, 32
Mixing bowls, 6
Mozzarella cheese
Caprese Salad Skewers, 157
Cauliflower & Ricotta
Pizza, 89–90
Chicken
Saltimbocca, 164–165
Creamy Tomato &
Sausage Rigatoni, 82–83
Homemade Pizza
Rolls, 62–63
Loaf Pan Eggplant
Lasagna, 93–94
Spinach Artichoke
Dip, 58–59

Mug Brownies à la Mode, 116
Multi-cookers, 3–4
Mushrooms
    Beef Wellington
        Bites, 126–127
    Easy Chicken & Shiitake
        Ramen, 69
Mussels in White Wine &
    Garlic with Crusty
    Bread, 96–97

N
Noodles. *See also* Pasta
    Easy Chicken & Shiitake
        Ramen, 69
    Shrimp Pad Thai, 100–101
Nut Free
    Adult Lemonade, 155
    Aperol Spritz, 160
    Apple Cinnamon
        Tartlets, 177
    Bacon-Wrapped Dates, 123
    Baked Lobster
        Macaroni &
        Cheese, 102–103
    Beef Wellington
        Bites, 126–127
    Blue Cheese-Stuffed
        Olives, 122
    Bourbon & Peach Tea
        Punch, 131
    Bread Pudding for Two, 107
    Breakfast Sandwiches
        on Toasted
        Brioche, 28–29
    Brussels Sprouts
        Gratin, 172–173
    Buffalo Chicken
        Meatballs, 64
    Burrata & Fig Crostini, 169
    Cacio e Pepe, 91–92
    Caprese Salad Skewers, 157
    Caramelized Onion Dip, 147

Caramelized Shallot &
    Garlic Mashed
    Potatoes, 174
Carbonara Risotto, 80–81
Carnitas Tacos with
    Pickled Red Onion &
    Slaw, 76–77
Cauliflower & Ricotta
    Pizza, 89–90
Chicken & Chickpea Tikka
    Masala, 70–71
Chicken
    Saltimbocca, 164–165
Chili Roasted Sweet
    Potatoes, 52
Chocolate Cake with
    Buttercream
    Frosting, 142–143
Chocolate Chip Skillet
    Cookie, 119
Chocolate Mousse, 106
Chopped Kale Greek
    Salad, 44
Classic Beef Stew, 78–79
Coconut Sticky Rice, 53–54
Cod and Vegetables en
    Papillote, 98
Coffee Cake Muffins, 137
Coffee Crème
    Brûlée, 108–109
Corn Bread Muffins, 55
Cranberry & Brie Bites, 170
Cranberry Mule, 178
Creamy Sun-Dried Tomato
    Chicken Pasta, 74–75
Creamy Tomato &
    Sausage Rigatoni, 82–83
Creamy Tomato Soup, 56
Crispy Garlic Green
    Beans, 49
Deviled Eggs, 146
Easy Bacon & Broccoli
    Strata, 138

Eggs & Bacon Fried
    Rice, 26–27
Eggs Benedict
    Florentine, 21–22
Elote Corn Salad, 149
Falafel Gyros with
    Tzatziki, 85–86
French Toast with Peaches
    and Honey, 35–36
Garlic & Herb Filet
    Mignon, 84
Garlic Sautéed Broccoli
    Rabe, 162
Giant Cinnamon Rolls, 37–39
Gochujang BBQ
    Chicken, 152
Grilled Chicken & Romaine
    Caesar, 42–43
Grilled Zucchini with
    Lemon Zest, 161
Homemade Burger
    Bar, 150–151
Homemade Crispy
    Waffles, 33–34
Homemade Pizza
    Rolls, 62–63
Honey Sriracha-Glazed
    Salmon, 95
Italian Cheese &
    Charcuterie Board, 158
Leftover Turkey Potpie
    Hand Pies, 179–181
Lemon-Rosemary Roasted
    Turkey, 175–176
Loaf Pan Eggplant
    Lasagna, 93–94
Mimosa Bar, 139
Mini Avocado & Ricotta
    Toasts, 135
Mini Cheesecakes, 114–115
Mixed Berry Dutch Baby, 32
Mug Brownies à la
    Mode, 116
Paloma Cocktails, 130

Nut Free (*Continued*)

Parmesan Roasted
Asparagus, 50

Peach & Raspberry
Cobbler, 112–113

Potato & Chorizo
Bites, 124–125

Prosciutto-Wrapped
Chicken, 68

Prosecco Ice Pops, 132

Roasted Asian-Style
Broccoli, 48

Roasted Rosemary
Potatoes, 51

Simple Fruit Salad, 136

Simple Tiramisu, 166

Southwest Chicken &
Avocado Salad, 46–47

Spicy Chicken Bites, 65

Spinach Artichoke
Dip, 58–59

Sprinkle-Loaded Waffles, 141

Strawberry-Basil Sorbet, 105

Strawberry
Shortcake, 110–111

Thai Red Curry
Chicken, 72–73

Tomato, Spinach & Goat
Cheese Omelets, 24–25

Tomato & Bacon Grilled
Cheese, 66

Tzatziki, 184

Watermelon & Feta
Salad, 148

White Bean Hummus, 57

Nuts

Chocolate-Hazelnut
Spread, 183

Homemade Granola &
Yogurt Parfait, 20

Prosciutto & Pear Arugula
Salad, 41

Shrimp Pad Thai, 100–101

O

Oats

Homemade Granola &
Yogurt Parfait, 20

Olives

Blue Cheese-Stuffed
Olives, 122

Chopped Kale Greek
Salad, 44

Italian Cheese &
Charcuterie Board, 158

One Pot

Aperol Spritz, 160

Apple Cinnamon
Tartlets, 177

Bacon-Wrapped Dates, 123

Bourbon & Peach Tea
Punch, 131

Breakfast Sandwiches on
Toasted Brioche, 28–29

Burrata & Fig Crostini, 169

Caprese Salad Skewers, 157

Chili Roasted Sweet
Potatoes, 52

Chopped Kale Greek
Salad, 44

Classic Beef Stew, 78–79

Cod & Vegetables en
Papillote, 98

Cranberry Mule, 178

Creamy Tomato Soup, 56

Easy Chicken & Shiitake
Ramen, 69

5-Ingredient Pesto, 185

Garlic Sautéed Broccoli
Rabe, 162

Lemon-Rosemary Roasted
Turkey, 175–176

Mug Brownies à la
Mode, 116

Mussels in White Wine &
Garlic with Crusty
Bread, 96–97

Paloma Cocktails, 130

Parmesan Roasted
Asparagus, 50

Peanut Butter Cup
S'mores, 154

Roasted Rosemary
Potatoes, 51

Strawberry-Basil Sorbet, 105

Thai Red Curry
Chicken, 72–73

Tomato Tart with
Burrata, 61

Trofie al Pesto, 163

White Bean Hummus, 57

Onions

Caramelized Onion Dip, 147

Carbonara Risotto, 80–81

Carnitas Tacos with Pickled
Red Onion & Slaw, 76–77

Chopped Kale Greek
Salad, 44

Classic Beef Stew, 78–79

Creamy Tomato Soup, 56

Eggs & Bacon Fried
Rice, 26–27

Falafel Gyros with
Tzatziki, 85–86

Gochujang BBQ
Chicken, 152

Leftover Turkey Potpie
Hand Pies, 179–181

Lemon-Rosemary Roasted
Turkey, 175–176

Loaf Pan Eggplant
Lasagna, 93–94

Mussels in White Wine &
Garlic with Crusty
Bread, 96–97

Potato & Chorizo
Bites, 124–125

Simple Asian Salad with
Ginger Dressing, 45

Organization, 7–8

P

Paloma Cocktails, 130

Pancetta

Carbonara Risotto, 80–81

Pantry staples, 8–9

Parmesan cheese

Baked Lobster Macaroni & Cheese, 102–103

Brussels Sprouts Gratin, 172–173

Carbonara Risotto, 80–81

Cauliflower & Ricotta Pizza, 89–90

Creamy Sun-Dried Tomato Chicken Pasta, 74–75

Creamy Tomato & Sausage Rigatoni, 82–83

5-Ingredient Pesto, 185

Grilled Chicken & Romaine Caesar, 42–43

Homemade Pizza Rolls, 62–63

Loaf Pan Eggplant Lasagna, 93–94

Parmesan Roasted Asparagus, 50

Spinach Artichoke Dip, 58–59

Summer Veggie Orecchiette and Pesto, 87–88

Parmesan Roasted Asparagus, 50

Parmigiano-Reggiano cheese

Cacio e Pepe, 91–92

Italian Cheese & Charcuterie Board, 158

Parsley

Creamy Tomato & Sausage Rigatoni, 82–83

Falafel Gyros with Tzatziki, 85–86

Loaf Pan Eggplant Lasagna, 93–94

Mussels in White Wine & Garlic with Crusty Bread, 96–97

Parsnips

Classic Beef Stew, 78–79

Parties, 120–121

Birthday Brunch, 134–144

cocktail, 12, 121–131

dinner, 13, 156–166

Friendsgiving Feast, 168–181

planning, 14

Weekend BBQ, 146–155

Pasta

Baked Lobster Macaroni & Cheese, 102–103

Cacio e Pepe, 91–92

Creamy Sun-Dried Tomato Chicken Pasta, 74–75

Creamy Tomato & Sausage Rigatoni, 82–83

Summer Veggie Orecchiette and Pesto, 87–88

Trofie al Pesto, 163

Peaches

Bourbon & Peach Tea Punch, 131

French Toast with Peaches and Honey, 35–36

Mimosa Bar, 139

Peach & Raspberry Cobbler, 112–113

Peanut Butter Cup S'mores, 154

Pears

Prosciutto & Pear Arugula Salad, 41

Peas

Eggs & Bacon Fried Rice, 26–27

Leftover Turkey Potpie Hand Pies, 179–181

Summer Veggie Orecchiette & Pesto, 87–88

Pecorino Romano cheese

Cacio e Pepe, 91–92

Pepperoni

Homemade Pizza Rolls, 62–63

Peppers

Thai Red Curry Chicken, 72–73

Perfect Grazing Board, The, 128–129

Pesto, 5-Ingredient, 185

Summer Veggie Orecchiette and Pesto, 87–88

Tomato Tart with Burrata, 61

Trofie al Pesto, 163

Pineapple

Simple Fruit Salad, 136

Pine nuts

5-Ingredient Pesto, 185

Pizza, Cauliflower & Ricotta, 89–90

Pizza Rolls, Homemade, 62–63

Pork. *See also* Bacon; Pancetta; Prosciutto; Sausage

Carnitas Tacos with Pickled Red Onion & Slaw, 76–77

Potatoes. *See also* Sweet potatoes

Caramelized Shallot & Garlic Mashed Potatoes, 174

Classic Beef Stew, 78–79

Potato & Chorizo Bites, 124–125

Roasted Rosemary Potatoes, 51

Pots and pans, 4, 6

Prosciutto
  Chicken
    Saltimbocca, 164–165
  Italian Cheese &
    Charcuterie Board, 158
  Prosciutto & Pear Arugula
    Salad, 41
  Prosciutto-Wrapped
    Chicken, 68
Prosecco Ice Pops, 132
Provolone cheese
  Creamy Tomato &
    Sausage Rigatoni, 82–83
  Italian Cheese and
    Charcuterie Board, 158
Pumpkin Spice Iced Coffee, 144

R

Radishes
  Mini Avocado & Ricotta
    Toasts, 135
Recipes, about, 15–17
Registry, 2–6
Rice
  Carbonara Risotto, 80–81
  Chicken & Chickpea Tikka
    Masala, 70–71
  Coconut Sticky Rice, 53–54
  Eggs & Bacon Fried
    Rice, 26–27
  Thai Red Curry
    Chicken, 72–73
Ricotta cheese
  Cauliflower & Ricotta
    Pizza, 89–90
  Creamy Tomato &
    Sausage Rigatoni, 82–83
  Italian Cheese &
    Charcuterie Board, 158
  Loaf Pan Eggplant
    Lasagna, 93–94
  Mini Avocado & Ricotta
    Toasts, 135

Roasted Asian-Style
    Broccoli, 48
Roasted Rosemary Potatoes, 51
Rosemary
  Adult Lemonade, 155
  Beef Wellington
    Bites, 126–127
  Cod & Vegetables en
    Papillote, 98
  Garlic & Herb Filet
    Mignon, 84
  Lemon-Rosemary Roasted
    Turkey, 175–176
  Roasted Rosemary
    Potatoes, 51

S

Sage
  Chicken
    Saltimbocca, 164–165
Salads
  Caprese Salad Skewers, 157
  Chopped Kale Greek
    Salad, 44
  Elote Corn Salad, 149
  Grilled Chicken & Romaine
    Caesar, 42–43
  Prosciutto & Pear Arugula
    Salad, 41
  Simple Asian Salad with
    Ginger Dressing, 45
  Simple Fruit Salad, 136
  Southwest Chicken &
    Avocado Salad, 46–47
  Watermelon & Feta
    Salad, 148
Salmon, Honey
    Sriracha-Glazed, 95
Sausage
  Creamy Tomato &
    Sausage Rigatoni, 82–83
  Potato & Chorizo
    Bites, 124–125

Seafood. *See also* Fish
  Mussels in White Wine &
    Garlic with Crusty
    Bread, 96–97
  Shrimp Pad Thai, 100–101
Shrimp Pad Thai, 100–101
Simple Asian Salad with Ginger
    Dressing, 45
Simple Fruit Salad, 136
Simple Tiramisu, 166
Skillets, cast-iron, 2–3, 6
Soups and stews
  Classic Beef Stew, 78–79
  Creamy Tomato Soup, 56
  Easy Chicken & Shiitake
    Ramen, 69
Sour cream
  Caramelized Onion Dip, 147
  Caramelized Shallot &
    Garlic Mashed
    Potatoes, 174
  Mini Cheesecakes, 114–115
  Potato & Chorizo
    Bites, 124–125
Southwest Chicken & Avocado
    Salad, 46–47
Spicy Chicken Bites, 65
Spinach
  Eggs Benedict
    Florentine, 21–22
  Spinach Artichoke
    Dip, 58–59
  Tomato, Spinach & Goat
    Cheese Omelets, 24–25
Spinach Artichoke
    Dip, 58–59
Sprinkle-Loaded Waffles, 141
Stand mixers, 4, 5
Stockpots, 6
Stracciatella Semifreddo, 118
Strawberry-Basil Sorbet, 105
Strawberry Shortcake, 110–111

Summer Veggie Orecchiette & Pesto, 87–88

Sweet Potatoes, Chili Roasted, 52

T

Tacos, Carnitas, with Pickled Red Onion & Slaw, 76–77

Thai Red Curry Chicken, 72–73

Thanksgiving, 168–181

Thyme

Beef Wellington Bites, 126–127

Brussels Sprouts Gratin, 172–173

Garlic & Herb Filet Mignon, 84

Tomatoes

Breakfast Sandwiches on Toasted Brioche, 28–29

Caprese Salad Skewers, 157

Chopped Kale Greek Salad, 44

Creamy Tomato Soup, 56

Falafel Gyros with Tzatziki, 85–86

Southwest Chicken & Avocado Salad, 46–47

Summer Veggie Orecchiette & Pesto, 87–88

Tomato, Spinach & Goat Cheese Omelets, 24–25

Tomato & Bacon Grilled Cheese, 66

Tomato Tart with Burrata, 61

Tomatoes, sun-dried

Creamy Sun-Dried Tomato Chicken Pasta, 74–75

Trofie al Pesto, 163

Turkey

Leftover Turkey Potpie Hand Pies, 179–181

Lemon-Rosemary Roasted Turkey, 175–176

Tzatziki, 184

Falafel Gyros with Tzatziki, 85–86

W

Waffles

Homemade Crispy, 33–34

Sprinkle-Loaded, 141

Watermelon & Feta Salad, 148

Weekend BBQ, 146–155

Weeknight

Adult Lemonade, 155

Aperol Spritz, 160

Apple Cinnamon Tartlets, 177

Buffalo Chicken Meatballs, 64

Burrata & Fig Crostini, 169

Cacio e Pepe, 91–92

Caprese Salad Skewers, 157

Chocolate-Hazelnut Spread, 183

Chopped Kale Greek Salad, 44

Cod & Vegetables en Papillote, 98

Cranberry Mule, 178

Creamy Sun-Dried Tomato Chicken Pasta, 74–75

Creamy Tomato & Sausage Rigatoni, 82–83

Deviled Eggs, 146

Easy Chicken & Shiitake Ramen, 69

Elote Corn Salad, 149

Falafel Gyros with Tzatziki, 85–86

5-Ingredient Pesto, 185

Garlic & Herb Filet Mignon, 84

Garlic Sautéed Broccoli Rabe, 162

Grilled Chicken & Romaine Caesar, 42–43

Grilled Zucchini with Lemon Zest, 161

Homemade Burger Bar, 150–151

Italian Cheese & Charcuterie Board, 158

Mug Brownies à la Mode, 116

Mussels in White Wine & Garlic with Crusty Bread, 96–97

Peanut Butter Cup S'mores, 154

Prosciutto & Pear Arugula Salad, 41

Pumpkin Spice Iced Coffee, 144

Shrimp Pad Thai, 100–101

Simple Asian Salad with Ginger Dressing, 45

Simple Tiramisu, 166

Southwest Chicken & Avocado Salad, 46–47

Sprinkle-Loaded Waffles, 141

Strawberry Shortcake, 110–111

Summer Veggie Orecchiette & Pesto, 87–88

Thai Red Curry Chicken, 72–73

Tomato & Bacon Grilled Cheese, 66

Tomato Tart with Burrata, 61

Weeknight (*Continued*)

Trofie al Pesto, 163

Tzatziki, 184

Watermelon & Feta
Salad, 148

White Bean Hummus, 57

Wine glasses, 5

Y

Yogurt, Greek

Chicken & Chickpea
Tikka
Masala, 70–71

Homemade Granola &
Yogurt Parfait, 20

Spinach Artichoke
Dip, 58–59

Tzatziki, 184

Z

Zucchini, Grilled, with Lemon
Zest, 161

ACKNOWLEDGMENTS

To our family, thank you for your unwavering love and support throughout our journey together. We love each and every one of you.

To our dear friends, thank you for always cheering us on and traveling to Italy to celebrate our love story.

To Alex and Maddison, thank you for always being up for a dinner party, trying new recipes, and inspiring so many stories in this book.

To Bridget and our team at Callisto Media, thank you for all your time and patience throughout this entire process, and for your constant encouragement. We are so grateful to have had the experience of writing this book together.

Last, but not least, to you, our amazing readers, thank you for bringing us into your home as you learn to cook together! We hope you use this book and treasure these recipes for years to come!

ABOUT THE AUTHORS

KENZIE SWANHART is a home cook turned food blogger and cookbook author who provides inspiration to readers both in and out of the kitchen. With more than 150,000 copies of her cookbooks sold, Kenzie never wavers in her mission for her readers: creating and sharing easy yet flavorful recipes made with real ingredients.

As the head of culinary marketing and innovation for Ninja, a leading kitchen appliance company, Kenzie and her team provide a unique, food-first point of view for the development of new products and recipes to make consumers' lives easier and healthier. You'll also see her serving as the face of Ninja on the leading television home shopping network, where she shares tips, tricks, and recipes for the company's full line of products.

JULIEN LEVESQUE is a marketing and product development professional in the durable goods world—and a self-proclaimed foodie. Growing up in a family with several chefs and relatives who knew their way around the kitchen, Julien always had a penchant for cooking. Having taste-tested almost every recipe Kenzie has developed over the past nine years, he jumped at the chance to partner with her to bring this vision to life and share their love of food and cooking together with the world.

Kenzie and Julien live in Boston with their dog, Charlie.

CPSIA information can be obtained
at www.ICGtesting.com
Printed in the USA
BVHW090608160819
555789BV00001B/1